Computational
Texture and Patterns

From Textons to Deep Learning

Synthesis Lectures on Computer Vision

Editor
Gérard Medioni, *University of Southern California*
Sven Dickinson *University of Toronto*

Synthesis Lectures on Computer Vision is edited by Gérard Medioni of the University of Southern California and Sven Dickinson of the University of Toronto. The series publishes 50–150 page publications on topics pertaining to computer vision and pattern recognition. The scope will largely follow the purview of premier computer science conferences, such as ICCV, CVPR, and ECCV. Potential topics include, but not are limited to:

- Applications and Case Studies for Computer Vision

- Color, Illumination, and Texture

- Computational Photography and Video

- Early and Biologically-inspired Vision

- Face and Gesture Analysis

- Illumination and Reflectance Modeling

- Image-Based Modeling

- Image and Video Retrieval

- Medical Image Analysis

- Motion and Tracking

- Object Detection, Recognition, and Categorization

- Segmentation and Grouping

- Sensors

- Shape-from-X

- Stereo and Structure from Motion

- Shape Representation and Matching

- Statistical Methods and Learning

- Performance Evaluation

- Video Analysis and Event Recognition

Computational Texture and Patterns: From Textons to Deep Learning
Kristin J. Dana
2018

Probabilistic and Biologically Inspired Feature Representations
Michael Felsberg
2018

A Guide Convolutional Neural Networks for Computer Vision
Salman Khan, Hossein Rahmani, Syed Afaq, Ali Shah, and Mohammed Bennamoun
2018

Covariances in Computer Vision and Machine Learning
Hà Quang Minh and Vittorio Murino
2017

Elastic Shape Analysis of Three-Dimensional Objects
Ian H. Jermyn, Sebastian Kurtek, Hamid Laga, and Anuj Srivastava
2017

The Maximum Consensus Problem: Recent Algorithmic Advances
Tat-Jun Chin and David Suter
2017

Extreme Value Theory-Based Methods for Visual Recognition
Walter J. Scheirer
2017

Data Association for Multi-Object Visual Tracking
Margrit Betke and Zheng Wu
2016

Ellipse Fitting for Computer Vision: Implementation and Applications
Kenichi Kanatani, Yasuyuki Sugaya, and Yasushi Kanazawa
2016

Computational Methods for Integrating Vision and Language
Kobus Barnard
2016

Computational Texture and Patterns: From Textons to Deep Learning
Kristin J. Dana

ISBN: 978-3-031-00695-1   paperback
ISBN: 978-3-031-01823-7   ebook
ISBN: 978-3-031-00080-5   hardcover

DOI 10.1007/978-3-031-01823-7

A Publication in the Springer series
SYNTHESIS LECTURES ON COMPUTER VISION

Lecture #14
Series Editors: Gérard Medioni, *University of Southern California*
                Sven Dickinson *University of Toronto*
Series ISSN
Print 2153-1056   Electronic 2153-1064

Computational
Texture and Patterns

From Textons to Deep Learning

Kristin J. Dana
Rutgers University

SYNTHESIS LECTURES ON COMPUTER VISION #14

ABSTRACT

Visual pattern analysis is a fundamental tool in mining data for knowledge. Computational representations for patterns and texture allow us to summarize, store, compare, and label in order to learn about the physical world. Our ability to capture visual imagery with cameras and sensors has resulted in vast amounts of raw data, but using this information effectively in a task-specific manner requires sophisticated computational representations. We enumerate specific desirable traits for these representations: (1) intraclass invariance—to support recognition; (2) illumination and geometric invariance for robustness to imaging conditions; (3) support for prediction and synthesis to use the model to infer continuation of the pattern; (4) support for change detection to detect anomalies and perturbations; and (5) support for physics-based interpretation to infer system properties from appearance. In recent years, computer vision has undergone a metamorphosis with classic algorithms adapting to new trends in deep learning. This text provides a tour of algorithm evolution including pattern recognition, segmentation and synthesis. We consider the general relevance and prominence of visual pattern analysis and applications that rely on computational models.

KEYWORDS

texture, patterns, deep learning, machine learning, segmentation, synthesis, recognition, textons, style transfer

Contents

Preface

In recent years knowledge of image representations both in computers and in the brain has advanced significantly. While neural networks are not new, the concepts have returned at a time when computing resources can support the vast potential of these methods. This is an exciting time to learn, teach, invent, and discover. Patterns capture repetition and saliency in signals and representations of visual patterns allow us to concisely summarize what is important and to predict what's next. Raw data is too abundant for human parsing and a front-end pattern or texture analysis will likely be a requirement in multiple modern systems of the future such as automated driving, robot navigation, advanced manufacturing and 3D mapping. The intent of this text is to inspire and teach by first considering the beauty of patterns (Chapter 1); to consider classical texton-based methods of recognition (Chapter 2); to provide an introduction to deep learning for pattern recognition (Chapter 3); and to see how the past and the future have merged to change not only recognition but also segmentation (Chapter 4), synthesis (Chapter 5), and style transfer (Chapter 6). Modern representations that are multiscale and multilayer have some similar properties to the simpler, yet powerful, image pyramid representations. Chapter 7 discusses the return of the pyramid as a popular component in algorithms. Open issues in computational representations of patterns are discussed in Chapter 8. Chapter 9 addresses the question of *Why study texture?* by providing numerous real-world application examples that use or will use these methods. Chapter 10 provides an overview of the cloud-based computational resources and machine learning libraries that will power this future of data-centric algorithms. This text is not comprehensive but is meant to be read as an accompaniment to the literature which can be vast and unwieldy to traverse without context. This text may be viewed as a tour in which the reader gets a scaffolding of knowledge that serves as a starting point for more exploration.

Kristin J. Dana
June 2018

Acknowledgments

Thank you to all who have helped and have been inspirational in this work. Special thanks to my students including Hang Zhang, Parneet Kaur, Eric Wengrowski, Jia Xue, Matthew Purri, and Thomas Shyr, and student-turned-colleague Oana Gabriela Cula. I also acknowledge my mentors during my undergraduate and graduate education who set excellent examples of mentoring: Shree Nayar (Columbia), Thomas Weiss (MIT), Dennis Freeman (MIT), Jakub Segen (Bell Laboratories), and C. Marc Bastuscheck (NYU Robotics Lab). And great thanks to my husband, to my children and to my entire family whom I love and cherish. I am grateful for the ability and opportunity to pursue knowledge.

Portions of this work have been supported by NSF research grants **IIS-1715195 and IIS-1421134**.

Kristin J. Dana
June 2018

CHAPTER 1

Visual Patterns and Texture

Patterns in nature are beautiful to behold and have been the subject of fascination for scientists and mathematicians, writers, photographers, and artists [1–3, 13, 25, 26, 81, 194]. Our intrigue with visual patterns has an analogy to the perception of a musical chord; the spatial arrangement of shades and colors gives an appealing perceptual impression. Digital imagery is now abundant in science, medicine, industry, business, and everyday life. Visual patterns are interesting not only because of their perceptual response, but also because algorithms can characterize and quantify patterns in novel and useful ways. For example, image compression uses patterns to efficiently summarize extensive content; biometric recognition use fingerprint patterns for identification and weather modeling uses atmospheric patterns to predict near-term weather. The repetitive nature of patterns, while often not exact, is a powerful computational tool. A key challenge is finding the best *computational representation* that can be employed in algorithms to detect and recognize patterns, to compare two patterns precisely, to monitor or predict pattern change over time and to render similar patterns. Some of these goals can be partially achieved with current algorithms, but many open issues remain.

As motivation for the required sophistication of the representation we seek, consider the simple task of comparing two patterns. For the scene depicted in Figure 1.1, consider the question: *Are the two trees in this image the same tree type?* This is a more challenging question than simply asking whether there is a tree in the image. Humans have little trouble answering such a question indicating that the brain builds a pattern representation that can be used for similarity assessment. Suppose we further ask the question: *Has the health of these trees changed since last year?* A specially trained scientist like a botanist or dendrologist may be able to answer this question by inspecting the tree's appearance. But how would a computer algorithm approach the human expert's accuracy? Indeed, in many applications where appearance needs to be accurately assessed, a human expert is required. The digital age with abundant visual data creates the opportunity for real-world applications based on automated assessment of visual patterns.

While most papers on patterns and texture focus on specific applications, such as recognition or synthesis, it is interesting to take a more global view and address the key question: *What are the set of desired requirements for a computational representation for patterns or texture?* As with standard image representation (for objects, scenes and faces), texture models must have properties which support recognition in real-world conditions such as illumination and geometry invariance. However, for texture we are also interested in the unique property of *repetition* and the representation should characterize the distribution and variation of the repeating structure.

Figure 1.1: Consider a simple visual pattern of a tree with branches. While the human visual system can easily assess the visual pattern and determine that the trees are the same type, algorithms to do so are challenging. Furthermore, more fine-grained assessments of appearance such as *Has the health of these trees changed since last year?* are still open issues.

This type of representation is often referred to as an *orderless texture model*. Additionally, the ideal texture model may be used for methods beyond recognition (such as synthesis, segmentation, change detection) and the model should support these methods. Taking into account the list of desired attributes, we devise a set of texture model requirements/guidelines as follows.

1. **Intraclass Invariance** – to support recognition. All examples of the same texture class should give rise to similar representation values.

2. **Illumination and Geometric Invariance** – to support recognition in robust to real-world imaging conditions, i.e., changes in camera pose and environment illumination.

3. **Prediction and Synthesis** – to support texture synthesis given a model. Synthesizing texture based on the model indicates that the model captures the representation in a way that one can draw a sample from the underlying probability. When the synthesized texture is the continuation of an existing texture, the continuity between the existing sample and new sample must be consistent with the underlying model and is a prediction of the texture instance at a neighboring spatial grid location conditioned on the texture at the original spatial grid location. By capturing the nature of repeating structures, knowledge of large regions can be represented concisely. For time-varying texture or pattern models, the ability to predict is a temporal prediction where the model enables prediction of the future based on knowledge of the past.

4. **Gradient Computation** – to support detection of small changes, anomalies, and other perturbations. The direction of the gradient should be meaningful in a semantic context. (For example, a small texture change in a medical image may mean the early start of a disease. Conversely, a small texture change may mean the early response to a treatment. A small anomaly in a plant appearance may indicate the early start of crop failure.) Gradient computation with respect to texture representation is largely an open area of research.

5. **Physics-based Interpretation** – to support inference of physical properties from appearance. For example, predicting wind/weather patterns from water surface texture and predicting friction from surface reflectance. Physics from texture is also an open area of research.

This list of requirements comprises *texture model guidelines* by which to compare and contrast existing and prior models. A single model that exhibits all the requirements listed above remains an open research issue.

1.1   PATTERNS IN NATURE

When looking to nature and biology for inspiration on patterns, one may ask: *Is there a common framework for the generation of patterns in nature?* If so, this framework may provide a representation useful for other tasks beyond pattern generation. In prior research, real-world patterns have been modeled with fractals, diffusion processes, and cellular automata that have been shown to generate fascinating visual patterns that are replicated in nature.

Figure 1.2 shows animal patterns that can be modeled by a local reaction-diffusion process [202, 214] solved using nonlinear partial differential equations. Similarly, natural stripe patterns on a fish or wind patterns in sand have been found to be the minimization of a convex energy function [112]. Patterns of wind can be observed by transferring wind energy to visual patterns, as shown in Figure 1.3 which depicts an exhibit of free-flowing panels that deform in the wind creating a reflection pattern dependent on the spatial gradients of wind. Characterizing the symmetry of patterns [139] has important implications in computational patterns such as gait recognition with frieze patterns [127] and symmetry detection in urban scenes [234]. Examples of patterns in nature with symmetry are shown in Figure 1.4. Shapes may also take on characteristic patterns such as spirals in shells, the lattices in folding DNA, and the crystals of snowflakes. The Fibonacci spiral is visible in a hurricane vortex, a conch seashell, and a human ear, as shown in Figure 1.5. Fractal patterns are seen in tree branches or clouds, as shown in Figure 1.6. We are most interested in mathematical texture models that can generalize beyond specific fractal patterns or Fibonacci patterns. That is, we seek a mathematical framework and representation that can characterize general texture and serve as input to analysis algorithms. Traditionally, statistical models such as markov random fields have shown great utility in modeling texture. But more recently, deep learning has emerged as a powerful tool for modeling, outperforming traditional analytical, statistical and physics-based models. The notion of texture implies the need for an orderless representation where structure is repeated and the spatial ordering at some scale is not important. Deep learning representations for texture include deep filter banks [37], Fisher Vector CNN [36], Texture Networks for style transfer [205], and Deep Texture Encoding Networks [223]. Both classic and modern texture models for recognition, segmentation, and synthesis are described in subsequent chapters. As texture methods move from traditional to modern deep learning methods, researchers still face the fundamental problem of finding the best computational texture representation for a given task.

Figure 1.2: Diffusion processes can explain patterns in nature such as fur patterns on giraffes and tigers.

Figure 1.3: The pattern of wind as visualized on an array of oriented planar patches (on display at The Franklin Institute, Philadelphia, PA).

1.2 BIG DATA PATTERNS

Patterns and texture provide a way to cognitively summarize the scenes we see similar to the way names of objects and people are used to describe the things we see. Often these patterns and textures add adjectives to the objects, as in "striped zebra," "furry bear," "rough brick," and "spotted turtle." The patterns and textures in an image refer to the distribution of the visual primitives and the repetition in some manner over an image. The packaging of the visual elements in a single texture descriptor provides a great computational advantage. The representation doesn't represent the details, the individual blades of grass, grains of sand, or other primitive. Instead, large swatches of the image can be characterized or summarized with semantic labels. The im-

Figure 1.4: Symmetric patterns in design and nature.

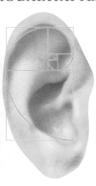

Figure 1.5: Fibonacci patterns in nature: a seashell, hurricane vortex, and a human ear. These patterns can be described by the Fibonacci sequence.

portance of scale here is evident; from a distance people in a crowd form a pattern, up-close the details of the individual are more relevant.

There is evidence that our human brain summarizes visual scenes using texture representations [5, 9, 35, 80]. It is unlikely that we can look at a tree and then sketch the exact distribution of branches. However, we may be able to sketch a similar distribution. Humans don't see the example placements of blades of grass, but they infer and retain the overall pattern. With the rise of big data, especially from image and video sources, modeling visual patterns is increasingly vital. Automated processing is needed to reduce raw data and obtain useful knowledge of imagery instead of storing the original pixel values. Although storage and computational power is large compared to prior years, imagery and video can overwhelm computing capacity when applied to the world at large. All data cannot be stored in its raw form because the amount of data becomes impractically cumbersome. Although it is easy to capture a photo, storing high-resolution, high-dynamic range, full-color images for every scene angle at every moment in time quickly yields unwieldy processing and storage requirements. Moving from data to knowledge onsite at the moment of image capture is increasingly important. Much of the signal variation within an image can be attributed to texture. Some of this is merely a background texture and the specifics are not important. For example, scene backgrounds can often be summarized by a texture descriptor and only the coefficients of the model need to be stored. Texture analysis and modeling provides a means to summarize scenes and find trends or changes. Texture models give a compact representation to determine identity, change and perceptual attributes (soft, scratchy, cold, hard) that can affect the action we take (grasping mechanism, or more task specific actions).

Figure 1.6: Fractal Patterns in nature: foliage (top) and clouds (bottom).

1.3   TEMPORAL PATTERNS

In some cases, pattern summarization needs to retain subtle but important detail. For example: the appearance of a fruit surface may indicate whether there is the start of decay; the surface appearance of sheet metal may indicate whether the manufacturing process over time continues to yield high quality; the temporal change of a skin rash appearance may indicate whether an allergic reaction is increasing or decreasing in intensity. For these applications, quantification of appearance to enable comparisons over time is essential. Humans can compare texture, especially if they are trained experts in a particular visual assessment (e.g., dermatologists making a diagnosis, artists creating a painting, interior designers evaluating textile aesthetics, and jewelers assessing value). Modeling texture and patterns recasts subjective appearance observed by humans into an objective quantifiable task that can be integrating in modern intelligent systems.

1.4   ORGANIZATION

In this text, we explore the use of computational modeling for visual patterns or texture (using the terms *patterns* and *texture* interchangeably). We explore representations that adhere to some of the *texture model guidelines*, as outlined in this chapter, to facilitate their use in algorithms. We compare and contrast classical work with modern methods using deep learning. We explore methods for visual patterns starting with classical work on textons in human vision and computational recognition. Specific algorithm domains such as texture segmentation, recognition and synthesis are described by starting with foundational knowledge of classic computer vision and then moving to modern advances of deep learning.

SUMMARY

In this chapter we have discussed visual patterns and texture and the need for a computational representation for algorithms. Patterns are interesting not only for their beauty but also because they give a means to summarize extensive content, look for anomalies, and predict change. Finding the right computational representation is challenging and is often dependent on the task at hand. We introduce texture model guidelines for comparing and contrasting computational models.

PROBLEMS

Explore the challenge of building texture/patten models, i.e., computational representations of texture, for algorithms such as recognition.

1.1.   Obtain images of a textured surface in a manner that you can control both the illumination direction (e.g., with a handheld light) and viewing direction (e.g., with a handheld camera). Begin by collecting three images of a surface texture from three different illumination direction. These images (Group 1) enable exploration of illumination invariance. Next, collect three images of a surface texture at three different viewing angles (frontal, 45°, and 70°). These images (Group 2) enable exploration of geometric or pose invariance. Finally, collect ten images of three classes of surface texture (e.g., grass, foliage, leaves, pebbles). These images (Group 3) enable exploration of intraclass invariance.

1.2.   *Intensity Distributions via histograms.* For each group of images evaluate the gray-scale intensity histogram and comment on this representations utility for recognition. Specifically discuss the merits or drawbacks of the representation with respect to illumination invariance, pose invariance, and intraclass invariance.

1.3.   *Fourier Coefficients* One early representation was based on the signal energy in spatial frequency bands as computed by computing a 2D fourier transform (FFT) of the image. Explore this representation by building code to: (1) read in an image and (2) preprocess the image by subtracting the dc value and multiplying by a 2D Hamming window. (3) Compute the log magnitude of the fourier transform. (4) Shift the 2D fourier transform so that zero frequency is centered. (4) Display the original image and the fourier transform.

    (a) Repeat the previous problem with the other texture images of Group 1 (different illumination angles). Describe the effect of changing the illumination direction on the FFT magnitude.

    (b) Repeat the previous problem with the other texture images of Group 2 (different viewing angles). Describe the effect of changing the illumination direction on the FFT magnitude.

    (c) From observations, is the FFT a good texture model/representation? Consider the properties of invariance in your response.

CHAPTER 2

Textons in Human and Computer Vision

In this chapter we give a concise tour of the path of scientific research that has grown from classical textons to modern deep learning. We will see that the current deep learning architectures have echos of past research incorporating orientation, scale space, and hierarchical models of processing.

2.1 PRE-ATTENTIVE VISION

In understanding general computational patterns, it is instructive to consider the human visual system's remarkable ability to represent and utilize image texture. Image texture is an intensity pattern that is a function of spatial coordinates and a color channel. The human brain excels at discriminating patterns (e.g., foreground pattern from background pattern). While our emphasis in this text is not specifically human vision, the mechanism of texture analysis in human vision provides insights for algorithms that quickly detect interesting patterns in large fields of data. Human visual pattern analysis can inspire fast and effective computer algorithms for both visual and non-visual patterns. Our intuition tells us that a human need not store and remember the exact placement of every leaf when seeing a textured region, as shown Figure 2.1. Instead, a quick scan of the scene indicates that there are textured regions and the geometric shape of these regions. Indeed there is significant scientific evidence, for a two-stage vision model. *Pre-attentive vision* summarizes the textured region as containing the same content, and differentiates that region from the differently textured background. In this pre-attentive mode, the human visual system processes the entire spatial region in parallel extracting features and making a quick analysis for segmentation and motion estimation. The second stage *attentive vision* is more precise and takes more processing time. This dichotomy between pre-attentive and attentive vision has been studied decades ago by several authors [20, 21, 104, 151, 201]. The pre-attentive stage is global but not precise, while the attentive stage has a small spatial focus region and can analyze in more detail. For general computational patterns beyond image texture, this mechanism is clearly attractive: large amounts of data can be processed in a "quick-scan" mode to find the important regions to focus attention.

Figure 2.1: Natural image texture. The human visual system is remarkably good at discriminating among textures and segmenting regions of similar texture.

2.2   TEXTON: THE EARLY DEFINITION

In the original invocation of the word *texton* by Julesz [103], the concept was used to explain the "pop-out" effect, i.e., spontaneous segregation of some textured regions, but not others. Consider that Figure 2.2 depicts a region of clearly discernible texture of the "+" symbol in a background of L's. On careful inspection of the background region one observes that it is comprised of both L's and T's. A region comprised of T's can be segmented from the region with L's, but the task is not as fast and requires more careful inspection. Pre-attentive vision can instantly segment, without detailed local analysis of how the image features formed structure. A closer inspection is needed to perceive the construct of the local element and therefore discriminate the letter types. It was originally hypothesized by Julesz that if the second-order image statistics of an image region varied, then spontaneous segmentation would occur. However, after many counterexamples were found, Julesz formulated the concept of textons. In the original texton work, a local configuration of image features (e.g., lines and junctions) comprise a texton and when the density of textons changes, the region can be segmented by pre-attentive vision.

Many of the early textons tests were done with contrived texture elements such as Figure 2.2 that did not resemble natural texture as in Figure 2.1. In order to model textures in real-world scenes, the concept of textons changed to a more computational representation that

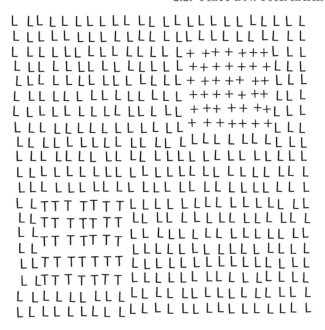

Figure 2.2: Spontaneous segregation of the textured regions with "+" is observable. Closer inspection is needed to perceive the construct of the local element and therefore discriminate the letter types to see the "T" region.

still embodied the notion of textons as having certain edge features and orientations. Specifically, image filtering using convolutions of the images with a set of filters, i.e., a filter bank, was used as a feature extraction step. The texton was represented by the filter bank output. The concept of texton was later refined to be the grouped or *clustered* filter outputs obtained from convolving an image with a set of filters [150].

The image filters used for feature extraction in traditional models are inspired by biological vision to be both multiscale and multiorientation. There is significant evidence that the human visual system performs a feature analysis or feature detection as the initial stage in the pipeline of visual processing. Gabor filters were a popular selection for computing features since Gabor models had been explored to model receptive fields in the visual cortex [66, 100, 203]. The Gabor model shows frequency selection of the receptive fields that are tuned in orientation and scale; specific neurons map to particular orientations (e.g., horizontal edge detectors, vertical edge detectors). Similarly, the features are tuned to a particular scale. However, Gaussian kernels are chosen for many desirable characteristics [113, 150, 215]. They are easy to approximate with discrete kernels as popularized in the pyramid image structure [163], a fundamental tool that enables real-time image processing for many algorithms. The Gaussian kernel is separable for efficient convolutions and easily approximated by the integer valued separable filter [1 4 6 4 1].

Furthermore, when comparing Gabor filters and Gaussian filters for modeling the response of the monkey striate cortex [220], the responses were found to be better matched by Gaussian filtering. Also during this time period, Gaussian filtering was studied in multiple contexts in signal processing.

In describing images in terms of features, the concept of scale plays an integral role. Consider the image set as shown in Figure 2.3 illustrating Monet's painting *Water Lilies* at three different scales. At fine scale, corresponding to a close-up view, the image features are details such as the artist's brushstrokes. Global structural detail is not evident in this view. The edges and contours of the lily pads and flowers are more readily apparent at a coarse scale (the more distant view). Image structures tend to have a characteristic scale.

Figure 2.3: Monet's water lilies at three different scales. (Left) brush strokes are evident but overall shape is unclear. (Center) Overall shape and edges are more apparent. (Right) Shape of lillies and scene are apparent.

As an example of the mechanics of feature extraction, consider edge detection at multiple scales. The process is done by convolving with a spatial blurring filter followed by a gradient filter such as [-0.5 0 0.5] to detect horizontal edges. Edges occur in locations of first derivative extrema, i.e., maxima of the gradient filtered images. Blurring the image *just enough* enables edge detection at a particular scale, but blurring too much destroys the structure of the edge and the region becomes a constant mean value. Image structures (edges, or first derivative extrema) exist at an optimal scale. Let scale space be denoted as the image blurred with a sequence of σ values so that we can parameterize a blurred image $blur(i(x,y))$ as $i(x,y,\sigma)$ where the blurring kernel is Gaussian with a standard deviation σ. Let $i'(x,y,\sigma)$ denote the convolution of the gradient filter with $i(x,y,\sigma)$, which gives an approximation of the derivative of i with respect to x for the horizonal gradient filter (and with respect to y for the vertical gradient filter). An edge occurs at a pixel if it is an extrema point. Therefore x,y is an edge pixel if $i'(x,y,\sigma) \geq i'(x+1,y,\sigma)$ and $i'(x,y,\sigma) \geq i'(x-1,y,\sigma)$. In practice, a reasonable ϵ is used making the condition $i(x,y,\sigma) - i'(x+1,y,\sigma) \geq \epsilon$ and $i(x,y,\sigma) - i'(x-1,y,\sigma) \geq \epsilon$. The edge will exist at a particular scale σ (and for all) finer scales. If we employ an image pyramid, downsampling is done for each coarser scale. That is, the image pyramid at level 0 is the original image $i(x,y)$ and the next level is obtained by blurring followed by downsampling (retaining every other pixel in the horizontal and vertical direction). For this multiresolution representation, the gradient filter (such as [-0.5 0 0.5]) operates on a larger effective region in the original image. (The intensity difference is computed between pixels that are 3 pixels apart instead of 1 pixel.) For the pyramid representation, edges can exist at a characteristic scale or set of scales and not for coarser of finer scales. Key point detectors such as SIFT [141] detect interest points that are more general than edges and they do so by looking at maxima in an image pyramid that are both spatial maxima and scale-space maxima.

Traditionally, scale space is a family of images that can be modeled by the diffusion equation [113] and no spurious detail (no new image structure) is generated by Gaussian blurring as the resolution decreases. Consider any 1D signal and its scale space, i.e., consider a series of blurrings of the signal parameterized by the standard deviation of the Gaussian blurring filter σ. As σ increases, no new extrema appear. However, as σ decreases, new extrema appear. This property makes scale space structure well behaved and easier to analyze. Additionally, the Gaussian kernel is readily differentiated so $I(x) = i(x) * g(x, \sigma)$ has an nth derivative given by

$$\frac{\partial^n I}{\partial x^n} = i * \frac{\partial^n g}{\partial x^n}. \tag{2.1}$$

Continuous scale space and the mathematical tools of differential geometry enables important results on invariants [65, 170].

By expanding the image into a scale space (or image pyramids) and computing numerous derivatives, intuition may tell us that using the raw signal is somehow easier than this expanded representation. However, by detecting extrema the representation encodes meaningful structure compactly and in a manner that supports invariants. For example, in object recognition invariance to lighting is important and image gradients provide some of this invariance because the gradient is indepedent of the overall brightness level. For geometric or pose invariance (recognizing objects and textures independent of the camera's point of view), representations which extract features and pool features can be used for geometric invariant representations, where raw image pixels are confounded by the effect of pose. In general, creating feature maps from images is a powerfool tool that enables image manipulations with algorithms that would not be possible with raw pixel values.

2.3   WHAT ARE TEXTONS? THEN AND NOW

As discussed in the previous section, the concept of a texton evolved from it's the early definition of a local configuration of lines and junctions to the filter-based texton definition. In the latter, the convolution outputs from a series of filters is the intermediate image representation. Although this intermediate representation is larger than the original image (e.g., a $w \times h$ image convolved with 9 filters and retaining the original size is $w \times h \times 9$), each filter output is describing a region, so a $p \times q$ image region or patch is now described by 9 filter outputs. Furthermore, since these filter outputs are quantized (e.g., by kmeans clustering) to a set of labels, or grouping of filter outputs. These groups or cluster centroids are referred to as textons and the collection of cluster centroids comprise a *texton dictionary* . Note that in image recognition, the visual words in the bag-of-words algorithm are analogous to textons. The histogram or distribution of textons is a representation of image texture. Comparing two textures is a task of comparing two texton histograms. To improve the representation, the texton histograms are often created using soft-weighting. That is, for a given pixel the M closest centroids are found (by comparing the filter output at the pixel with the filter output associated with each texton). Then each pixel is associated with M textons and a weight determined by the distance to the centroid. The histogram is created by summing a fractional contribution of each pixel to M bins. A key improvement to the texton histogram is to encode not only the closest centroid, but also the residual between that centroid and all the others in the dictionary [6, 105].

Modern texture representations have incorporated deep learning and CNNs. The original CNN architectures were not designed for specifically for texture, but they have been modified in recent architectures to create *texture encoding networks*. Hand-engineered features and filter banks are replaced by pre-trained CNNs and BoWs are replaced by the robust residual encoders such as VLAD [101] and its probabilistic version FV [161]. For example, Cimpoi et al. [38] assembles a selection of features (SIFT, CNNs) with t encoders (VLAD, FV) for a texture network. Deep-TEN [229] is a texture encoding network that is the first end-to-end learnable texture encoding network that ports the entire dictionary learning and residual encoding pipeline into a single layer for CNN. This encoding layer can be used in numerous applications, e.g., it is a key component to a recent semantic segmentation nextwork *EncNet* [227].

Texture representations in deep learning are discussed further in subsequent chapters within the context of recognition, segmentation, synthesis, and style transfer.

PROBLEMS

2.1. Construct a filter bank for feature extraction as follows. Begin with three Gaussian filters each with difference standard deviations $\sigma_1, \sigma_2 = 2 * \sigma_1, \sigma_3 = 4 * \sigma_1$. Convolve each of these filters with a horizontal, vertical and diagonal gradient filter. The result will be a collection of nine filters.

2.2. Choose three texture images, convert to grayscale, and convolve with the filters from the previous question. Given the original image has dimensions $w \times h$. The resulting image has the dimension $w \times h \times 9$.

2.3. Use K-means clustering to filter the 9×1 feature vectors to $K = 50$ clusters. Label all of the pixels in each of the three images with the closest of K labels. Display this label map (texton map) with distinguishable colors, e.g., using the matlab command *distinguishable_colors()*. Describe how dominant visual structures are encoded by the texton labels.

CHAPTER 3

Texture Recognition

3.1 TRADITIONAL METHODS OF TEXTURE RECOGNITION

Recognition methods in computer vision for objects, scenes, and faces have achieved significant attention and success in recent years. An interesting question to pose: Is recognition of a generic scene different from texture recognition? Human vision studies [169] indicate that the initial recognition of a scene is done with a mechanism similar to texture recognition. The intuition is that texture representations summarize image regions because the details are not needed for recognition. For texture, the specific ordering of spatial structure is often unimportant for recognition. For example, ordering of elements is not needed for branches in a forest, sand grains on a beach, leaves in a piles, grapes in bunch, waves in an ocean. Additionally, since structures repeat, a summarization or aggregation is necessary for an efficient representation. Contrast this with the ordering of structural elements of a face, such as eyes, nose, mouth; or the structural elements a car such as doors, windows, and headlights. For non-textured objects, ordering of structural elements is a significant cue that should be preserved in the representation. For algorithm development, when a scene can be considered "orderless" and has repetition, the methods for texture recognition may be identical to the methods for scene recognition.

In classic texture recognition work, image features capture the spatial variation of image intensity. Image features are computed using image filtering with a set of filter banks followed by grouping or clustering the filter outputs into characteristic vectors called textons [44, 129, 150, 209] that describe the local intensity variation. As discussed in Chapter 2, the set of textons obtained from clustering is referred to as the *texton library*. Since repetition of the textons are expected, and an orderless representation is generally desirable for texture, textons are aggregated into a *texton histogram* as the representation for recognition. For a texton library with K textons obtained from clustering, every image pixel is assigned a label $l \in [1 \cdots K]$. The K texton histogram bins each record the number of pixels with the associated label. Pooling of features is accomplished by this texton histogram in order to characterize the distribution of local features in the textured region. Recognition is done by computing histogram distances among a set of representative histograms for M texture classes. Texton histograms are used as a model for classification by representing specific textures by their histograms. For unsupervised recognition, histograms of observed textures are clustered to form groups without labels. For supervised clustering, the texton histograms are a feature vector for use in any standard classifier such as nearest neighbors of support vector machines. In addition to textons representing outputs of filter banks everywhere on the image, features near sparse key points such as those detected with the SIFT algorithm are used in classic texture recognition [230].

Using texton histograms for texture recognition is very similar to using bag-of-feature methods [43, 122] for traditional object recognition. The two methods, texton histograms and bag-of-features, have slightly different inspirations and trajectories. The texton histograms evolved from textons in human vision studies that are approximated by filter outputs and clustered to create textons. The term "bag-of-features" for visual representations of scenes are inspired by "bag-of-words" in document retrieval. Both methods cluster image features (e.g., filter outputs, raw pixels, or SIFT descriptors) to create either textons or visual words. The histogram of these textons or visual words is then used to represent the image.

Variations of the traditional texton method represent multiresolution image structure. The texton histogram can be computed as a function of image scale for a multiresolution orderless representation. Classic methods use image pyramids [163] in order to build multiresolution histograms of image intensity as a feature for texture representation [82]. The joint probability of features at multiple resolutions is also a good representation for recognition [23]. Pyramid match kernels [79] use pyramids to compare features at multiresolution, or multiple pyramid levels. For bag-of-feature methods, multiresolution methods are used to create spatial pyramid matching [122] that preserve some spatial ordering by computing histograms with spatial bins and different pyramid levels. This spatial component provides better descriptive capability resulting in high-performance recognition of many scenes. Invariance to rotation [180] and affine invariance [123, 124] are incorporated in texture representations for recognition robustness. Rotation invariance is incorporated in the very popular local binary pattern (LBP) representation [157]. This method represents a distribution of local of binary patterns instead of a distribution of textons. The binary patterns are obtained by considering only the signs of local gradients instead of the magnitude. The pattern is obtained by operating on pre-defined local circular neighborhoods, and a minimum over a rotation is obtained in order to achieve rotation invariance. The histogram of binary patterns or LBP histogram is a simple and efficient texture representation with good classification performance.

Extensions of texton histograms capture the appearance of 3D texture that varies with viewing and illumination direction. Such extensions include: (1) *3D textons* [129] where the filter outputs as a function of viewing and illumination direction are clustered to give the 3D texton cluster center and (2) *Bidirectional Feature Histogram* [44, 45, 48] where the texton histogram varies as a function of viewing and illumination direction. Texture recognition methods for time-varying dynamic textures typically use linear dynamical systems [167, 178, 217].

While multiresolution filters are a common theme in most texture representations, it is interesting to see if the raw pixel values can be used directly. For example, [190] and [208] both eschew the filter output representation and use image patch pixels directly. Normalization of the pixels are important and the favored approach is to normalize patches to zero mean and unit variance. However, for most methods filter bank outputs allow the emphasis of key image gradients with reduction of noice and irrelevant information. In traditional approaches, these filter banks are fixed and therefore are not typically optimized for the particular task at hand.

The classic texton histogram is a representation where each pixel is assigned a single label. However, significant improvements in performance are achieved using soft-weighted texton histograms [119, 207]. In the soft-weighted approach the distance to N closest textons is computed and this $N \times 1$ residual vector is used to represent the pixel instead of a single texton label. The concept of computing a *distance* or *residual* to the cluster centers is a powerful approach that yields performance increase. More recent representations that use a similar approach include *Fisher vectors* (FVs), where Gaussian mixture models are used instead of k-means clustering. The FV encodes the residual and can be used for classification [160]. Similar to FV, VLAD (vector of locally aggregated descriptors) computes a residual vector for recognition [7, 101] and achieves high performance as a classifier.

In some classical texture models, characterizing statistical dependence of spatial neighbors of the texture leads to Markov Random Field (MRF) models. The MRF is a computational representation that lends itself naturally to a probabilistic framework since the extension of stochastic process on a multidimensional space (e.g., a 2D image instead of a 1D time sequence) is a random field. Each texture image is modeled as an instance of an underlying process. The Markov random fields truncate the relationship between neighbors to only immediate neighbors, enabling computational tractability. This texture model requires a definition of the texture measurement at a point (e.g., the output of filter banks) and the statistical process governing the entire texture image (e.g., the random field). Estimating the underlying probability distribution that relates neighboring elements can be done with density estimation techniques such as maximum entropy [238]. The *conditional random field* (CRF) [121, 191] is a variation of the MRF where the posterior is inferred directly. That is, with x as the observation and y as the label the CRF directly models $p(y|x)$. As such, the CRF is a discriminative model useful for recognition.

3.2   FROM TEXTONS TO DEEP LEARNING FOR RECOGNITION

Traditional texture recognition has a long history in mathematically modeling the structural and statistical elements of visual surface texture. However, no single hand-designed model has been sufficiently scalable and descriptive to capture the vast palette of textures in the real world. Although these methods have been useful for small databases with distinct textures, large databases with thousands of classes and fine-grained categories/classes that vary in a subtle manner are much more challenging. Deep learning has brought in a new era of texture recognition algorithms with numerous successful methods being developed in recent years. However, there are parallels to be drawn between traditional and modern deep learning methods and some important algorithmic components in the represensations remain the same. Image filtering is an important component of both representations, but with deep methods, the filter coefficients are learned. Multiresolution approaches of traditional methods have their analogy in multilayer networks of deep learning. Binarization is effective in local binary pattern (LBP) traditional representations and nonlinear activation functions are a key component of deep networks. The traditional *histogram of textons* is a spatial pooling operator and the pooling layers of deep networks retain spatial pooling. Many modern methods use residual encoding that evolved from fisher vectors and VLAD. Invariance that was handcrafted in prior methods is obtained in deep learning by the flexibility of multilayer approaches that can represent classification functions that enable geometric and photometric invariance. A major difference is the supervision during the low-level and mid-level feature learning, unlike the traditional methods that relied on unsupervised clustering, e.g., to create the texton library.

3.3   TEXTURE RECOGNITION WITH DEEP LEARNING

Prior to 2012, many computer vision researchers recognized tens to hundreds of classes with automated recognition systems. However, there were few realistic and meaningful applications that can be built with recognition of only few classes. With the introduction of the Imagenet challenge [55], thousands of classes using training from millions of internet images was the new challenge. Deep learning networks [115] met the challenge and were quickly refined [88] to the point where automated recognition with thousands of classes could be done as well as a human. Interestingly, deep learning was not a new concept, but rather a reformulation of the neural network approach developed in the 1980's [125]. Deep learning in the area of recognition has profoundly affected the field in a very short time. Within three years, it became the most popular approach in algorithm development in object recognition and it changed the direction of research in and beyond computer vision.

Object recognition has fundamental differences with pattern/texture recognition. As we discussed in Chapter 1, repetition and distribution are key characteristics of a pattern or texture. An image of an object provides a *signature* that uniquely identifies the object. A robust object recognition algorithm must be robust to intraclass variations of this object (e.g., different types of dogs would all be recognized as dogs) and to variations due to imaging parameters (camera, illumination). For patterns, the same robustness to intraclass variations and imaging variations is required. But for patterns, the representation depicts a distribution and therefore intrinsically must capture repeating structures in a meaningful and compact manner.

In modern texture representations, hand-engineered features and filter banks are replaced by pre-trained convolutional neural nets (CNNs). Additionally, the simple histograms are replaced by residual encoders such as and VLAD (vector of locally aggregated descriptors) [106] and FV [162] to more robustly represent feature distributions.

The CNNs trained for databases such as ImageNet have been optimized for extracting multiscale features of general object images. However, the utility of the pre-trained CNN has been demonstrated for recognition tasks beyond the initial dataset classes. One possibility of using pre-trained CNNs is to retrain only the top layers so that the CNN can be used to recognize different classes. For adapting pre-trained CNNs to texture recognition, a slightly different approach has been used. The spatial organization is less important in texture recognition than in object recognition; an orderless representation is desirable for texture. In a multilayer CNN the spatial order is typically represented in the higher layers and the low-level features are captured in the lower layers. Therefore the lower layers of the pre-trained CNN can be used as a feature detector, much like the filter-bank outputs in the texton histogram (or bag-of-features) representation. The adaption of a CNN to an orderless representation by combining VLAD with CNN features in a framework that uses patches at multiple scales to achieve a multiscale orderless pooling of deep features referred to as *MOP-CNN* [77]. This approach improves the invariance of CNN for scene and texture recognition. In [38], features from pre-trained CNNs are combined with robust residual encoders to achieve high-performance texture recognition. This representation is referred to as *FV-CNN* since it combines pre-trained CNN with Fisher vector (FV) encoders.

In texture modeling, there is a typical quandry of separating the "texture" part and the "object part." Indeed most scenes naturally have the two integrated, such as the image of a wood-grained table or a furry animal. When we discuss texture recognition, there are two main types. Recognition where the input is segregated texture (e.g., Curet and KTH) or recognition with texture in the wild [36] (such as opensurfaces [18] and Minc [19]). A pioneering work [196, 197] for separating an image into style components and content components employs bilinear models. Building on this work and incorporating deep learning, bilinear CNN [137, 138] models have been developed. The basic composition of the bilinear CNN model are two branches each containing CNNs that separate style and content.This model can be trained end-to-end and used as orderless texture representation. Interesting visualization of the internal features of such a bilinear CNN have been explored [136] by demonstrating the appearance of the inverse of the learned bilinear CNN indicating the power of the representation to capture appearance details.

A new framework for texture is the deep texture encoding network (Deep-TEN [229]) that uses end-to-end learning where the feature extraction, dictionary learning, and encoding representation are learned together in a single network. Compared to using pre-trained CNNs, this approach has the benefit of gradient information passing to each component during back propagation, tuning each component for the recognition task at hand. High-performance recognition results on several state-of-the-art databases are demonstrated using Deep-TEN.

3.4   MATERIAL RECOGNITION VS. TEXTURE RECOGNITION

The terms texture recognition and material recognition are sometimes used interchangeably but there is a fundamental difference. Texture recognition is typically a term that refers to the classification of *image texture*, i.e., the spatial pattern of measured intensities in an image. Typically, the physical interaction of the light and surface is ignored. However, for *material* recognition, we are concerned with labeling the material composition of a surface, based on observation of its reflectance. Surface reflectance is captured by a camera, and the measured intensity depends on environment lighting, camera position, and the surface geometry as well as the characteristics of the camera sensor.

Accounting for viewing and illumination angle, measurements of bidirectional reflectance function (BRDF) or bidirectional texture function (BTF) [52, 53] provide a dense sampling of surface appearance. Material recognition often uses properties of reflectance to determine material composition and will employ full or partial measurements of the BRDF [219, 225]. Recent surveys enumerate and evaluate devices and methods to capture angular variations of surface appearance [51, 84]. Radiometric or photometric calibration is needed to ensure that the captured image is a linear function of the observed intensity. For recognition using deep networks, large labeled datasets are important for training [18, 19]. However, many material datasets contain labels that are indicative of the object class instead of the material composition (e.g., carpet, mirror). A recent database which labels materials according to a materials-science taxonomy [182, 183] provides supervision for learning local representations of material appearance and integrating global context for precise pixelwise labeling of scene materials [181, 184]. For physics-based material recognition, observation of reflectance provides insight to physical properties of the surface. Beyond classification, recent methods have used patterns in reflected light to ascertain surface friction [226] and acoustics [158].

SUMMARY

In this chapter we have discussed texture recognition from traditional methods based on texton histograms to modern deep learning methods.

PROBLEMS

Deep Learning Exercises

3.1. Build a small texture database (30 images) with images of three texture classes and 10 instance per class. Texture class examples include grass, foliage, pebbles, linen, canvas, carpet, and wood. The class instances should have similar visual characteristics so that a simple algorithm can be used for recognition. Build a texton histogram for each image. Use 5 instances per class as part of the training set for *Nearest Neighbor Classification*. Use Euclidian histogram distance for finding the distances between the test histogram and the histograms of the training set. Find the accuracy by testing the remaining 15 images. Display examples of the training and test histograms and comment on the similarity or dissimilarity. Compute and report the per-class accuracy as the number of correctly recognized images per class divided by the total number of images per class.

3.2. Repeat the prior question, but evaluate different distance metrics, specifically chi-squared distance metric and histogram intersection. Additionally, evaluate the effect of using soft-weighted histograms.

3.3.   Using the publicly available code for Deep-TEN on GitHub (`https://github.com/zhanghang1989/Torch-Encoding-Layer`), test the recognition for the KTH texture database (`http://www.nada.kth.se/cvap/databases/kth-tips/`).

3.4.   Using the publicly available code for Deep Filter Banks on GitHub (`https://github.com/mcimpoi/deep-fbanks`), test the recognition for the KTH texture database.

CHAPTER 4

Texture Segmentation

Segmentation of computational patterns, whether in images or other data, provides precise localization and delineation of the patterned region. The output of the segmentation encodes each distinct region with a unique label that is typically illustrated with an image of the segmentation map where each region is colored according to its label. When segmentation is combined with recognition, each labeled region also has a *semantic label* indicating what object class (e.g., person, car, bird) is within the region. Segmentation of visual imagery has important utility in practice. Characteristics such as the size, shape, and precise location can be assessed and used for applications such as robotic grasping, automated driving, medical diagnosis, and surgical planning. In movie editing, actors and objects can be automatically removed from one scene and added to another. Color editing confined to particular objects can be easily accomplished with precise segmentation. In traffic analysis, individual cars can be segmented from a scene for counting or for position mapping. The characteristics of the pattern region such as size and shape may be of interest and can be assessed following segmentation. In medical images, a region to be surgically removed can be precisely localized, cells can be delineated and counted. Once a segmented region of a pattern is obtained, the characteristics of the region shape can enable accurate change detection. The region can be monitored for size and shape changes. In dermatology, growth of a mole can be monitored; in weather analysis the geographic extent of a storm can be quantified; in satellite analysis, the extent of forests, oceans, and other significant patterns can be evaluated. The utility of segmentation extends beyond visual imagery to applications such as financial markets to find the start and end time of a particular trend, weather analysis of atmospheric data to characterize and localize trends, and medical records to delineate disease trajectories.

4.1 TRADITIONAL METHODS OF TEXTURE SEGMENTATION

For segmentation, as in recognition, there is a trend in algorithm development where classic techniques are reworked to take advantage of the new deep learning frameworks that provide mechanisms for automatic learning over large data sets resulting in invariance and robustness that typically exceeds traditional techniques. In considering how deep learning has steered segmentation algorithm development, we discuss a sampling of traditional segmentation methods and describe the functionality of these methods in general terms. Then, we examine more recent methods that use prior algorithms as a foundation but incorporate deep architectures that typically achieves large improvements in functionality and robustness.

There are numerous traditional image segmentation algorithms and variations of these algorithms spanning decades of research. Since exhaustively covering the literature is beyond the scope of this chapter, a few core algorithms are chosen for insights of the large body of research. Examples of these algorithms include: graph-based spectral methods such as n-cuts, grab-cuts [24, 172, 188], mean-shift segmentation [39, 40], conditional random fields, and edge or contour-based methods [8].

4.1.1   GRAPH-BASED METHODS

The challenge in pointwise segmentation is achieving contiguous regions where all points are correctly labeled. Simple local heuristics such as color thresholding for segmentation fail in real-world conditions. Graph-based spectral methods begin with establishing an affinity matrix between elements in the image such as pixels. We will present a simplified view of this segmentation to impart intuition for the algorithm. More tutorial-style details can be found in [85, 210].

As an illustrative example, consider a 10×10 image (100 pixels) as shown in Figure 4.1a. The affinity matrix W is a matrix where each element $W(i, j)$ for pixel i, j is the affinity or similarity between pixel i and pixel j where $i, j \in [1, 100]$. The affinity measure varies from algorithm to algorithm, but a simple affinity measure is the inverse of a metric that combines euclidian distance D_{ij} between the pixels and color distance C_{ij} between the pixels intensities given by $\sqrt{(c_i - c_j)^T (c_i - c_j)}$ where c_i is the red, green, blue color triple for pixel i and c_j is defined similarly for pixel j. That is, the affinity metric can be $e^{-D_{ij}^2} e^{-C_{ij}^2}$ when $D_{ij} < r$ and 0 otherwise. The variable r defines the neighborhood region around a pixel. The affinity matrix is normalized so that the sum over each row or column is equal to one.

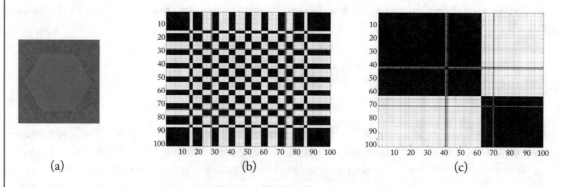

(a)   (b)   (c)

Figure 4.1: (a) A simple 10×10 image, (b) the 100×100 affinity matrix for this image, and (c) a reordered affinity matrix that can be achieved with spectral graph clustering such as Ncuts.

To see some basic intuition, consider that if we had a perfect affinity matrix that gave large affinities for pixels belonging to the same object/pattern/surface. In the simple 10×10 image of Figure 4.1a, the affinity matrix would look like Figure 4.1b. However, if we knew the ordering of pixels so that we could group pixels within the same region together, the affinity matrix would look like Figure 4.1c. The challenge in image segmentation is: *How does one find the ordering of pixels that reveal this block diagonal structure?* While we omit the proof here, spectral graph theory provides the answer. The Laplacian matrix L is given by $L = D - W$ where D is a diagonal degree matrix (with the ith diagonal element as the number of edges at node i) and W is the affinity matrix. The eigenvectors of this Laplacian matrix finds the ordering that reveals the block diagonal structure and consequently segments the image pixels.

We consider an illustrative example and use the adjacency matrix instead of the affinity matrix when computing L. Similar results apply to the affinity matrix in the graph Laplacian matrix. Consider the simple graph shown in Figure 4.2. Graphs are used to represent images with pixels as nodes and connections to neighboring pixels as edges. An adjacency matrix element $A(i, j) = 1$ if pixel i and pixel j are connected by an edge. For the example in Figure 4.2, the adjacency matrix is given in Figures 4.3 and 4.4.

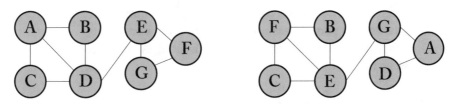

Figure 4.2: (Left) A simple graph. (Right) The same graph with the node labeling redistributed.

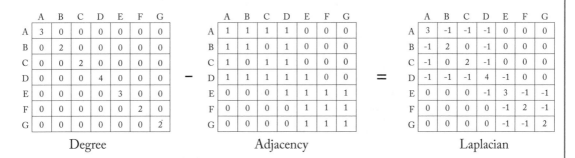

Figure 4.3: From the graph in Figure 4.2. The adjacency matrix (center) is subtracted from the degree matrix (left) to obtain the graph Laplacian (right). The second eigenvector of the graph Laplacian reveals the segments.

Note that the sum of each row of L is equal to zero since it is the degree of the pixel (node) minus the sum of all neighbors in its region. Therefore, we can identify an eigenvector of L as

	A	B	C	D	E	F	G
A	2	0	0	0	0	0	0
B	0	2	0	0	0	0	0
C	0	0	2	0	0	0	0
D	0	0	0	2	0	0	0
E	0	0	0	0	4	0	0
F	0	0	0	0	0	3	0
G	0	0	0	0	0	0	3

Degree

$-$

	A	B	C	D	E	F	G
A	0	0	0	1	0	0	1
B	0	0	0	0	1	1	0
C	0	0	0	0	1	1	0
D	1	0	0	0	0	1	0
E	0	1	1	0	0	1	1
F	0	1	1	0	1	0	0
G	1	0	0	1	1	0	0

Adjacency

$=$

	A	B	C	D	E	F	G
A	2	0	0	-1	0	0	-1
B	0	2	0	0	-1	-1	0
C	0	0	2	0	-1	-1	0
D	-1	0	0	2	0	-1	0
E	0	-1	-1	0	4	-1	-1
F	0	-1	-1	0	-1	3	0
G	-1	0	0	-1	-1	0	3

Laplacian

Figure 4.4: Illustration of the graph Laplacian from the graph in Figure 4.2 with nodes shuffled. The adjacency matrix is subtracted from the degree matrix to obtain the graph Laplacian. The second eigenvector of the graph Laplacian reveals the segments.

$x_1 = \mathbb{1}$ (the vector of ones) so that $Lx = \lambda_1 x$ and $\lambda_1 = 0$. The multiplicity of the zero eigenvalue is the number of connected components in the graph. Consider the second eigenvector x_2, that it is one for all the entries that correspond to pixels in the connected region, and zero otherwise, we again get the sum zero. This second eigenvector is a partitioning vector which assigns one to a component if that pixel is part of the region and zero otherwise.

For the example in Figure 4.3 the first two eigenvectors v_1 and v_2 computed with Matlab's *eigs* function is given by

$$v_1 = \begin{bmatrix} 0.3780 \\ 0.3780 \\ 0.3780 \\ 0.3780 \\ 0.3780 \\ 0.3780 \\ 0.3780 \end{bmatrix} \quad v_2 = \begin{bmatrix} 0.3560 \\ 0.3560 \\ 0.3560 \\ 0.2142 \\ -0.2966 \\ -0.4929 \\ -0.4929 \end{bmatrix}. \tag{4.1}$$

The first eigenvector is a scalar multiple of a vector of all ones and the second vector reveals the partitioning. In this case the nodes were already ordered. However, when the nodes are shuffled (Figures 4.2b and 4.4), the eigenvectors are as follows:

$$v_1 = \begin{bmatrix} 0.3780 \\ 0.3780 \\ 0.3780 \\ 0.3780 \\ 0.3780 \\ 0.3780 \\ 0.3780 \end{bmatrix} \quad v_2 = \begin{bmatrix} 0.6997 \\ -0.2094 \\ -0.2094 \\ 0.3966 \\ -0.0494 \\ -0.2094 \\ 0.4682 \end{bmatrix}. \tag{4.2}$$

The second eigenvector $v2$ again reveals the ordering. That is, clustering the values in the eigenvector shows two groups (nodes A,G,D in one group and the remainder in the other).

When computing the Laplacian matrix with affinity values instead of binary adjacency values, the graph has edges strengths, strong edges, and weak edges. Similarly, the second eigenvector of the image example in Figure 4.1 reveals the partitioning of the two regions of the image and was used to reorder the affinity matrix to the block diagonal structure shown in Figure 4.1c. The concepts of graph partitioning in segmentation has been used and refined in many algorithms included normalized cuts (n-cuts) [188], grab-cuts [24, 172], and multiscale spectral segmentation [42, 149].

4.1.2 MEAN SHIFT METHODS

Mean shift methods have become a computer vision mainstay algorithm due to robust performance and real-time operation [39, 40]. This method uses a shift operation from a starting point that converges to the mode of the region. The basic algorithm is elegantly straightfoward. For every point in the image, a window in feature space is considered and a mean value of the datapoints in this window computed. For example, the feature vector may be five-dimensional consisting of the x, y image coordinate and the r, g, b color triple. A window in this five-dimensional space is used to compute mean value of points within the window. When computing the mean, the values are often weighted by a Gaussian kernel weighting the central values more than the edge. In the next step the window is shifted to the mean value of the window region and the process is repeated until the mean converges to the region's mode. Each pixel in the image undergoes the mean-shift transformation and those pixels that converge to the same mode are grouped together in the segmentation. Examples of images segmented using mean shift are given in Figure 4.5. The efficiency and robustness of mean-shift led to its widespread use in both image segmentation and real-time object tracking.

4.1.3 MARKOV RANDOM FIELDS

Another direction for segmentation has been the use of MRF and CRFs [114, 121, 175, 191]. MRFs and CRFs are graph models for segmentation that represent pixels as nodes on a graph and links between nodes as probabilistic relationship between pixels. The labels of the pixels are the unknowns, often called *latent variables*. The pixel intensities are known and are considered the *observation*. The goal in segmentation can be stated as predicting the pixels label x given the observed intensity y. Knowing the conditional probability $p(x|y)$ helps this prediction, because the choice of the label x_i that maximizes this conditional probability is a logical good choice that is most likely given the observation. Additionally, neighboring pixels are inter-related, i.e., there is a high probability that two neighboring pixels belong to the same object or region. Therefore, the labels of two neighboring pixels are dependent and the label is dependent on the observation. We assume that when considering the label of a particular pixel, the neighborhood around the pixel affects the label prediction. Prediction of one label affects the prediction of the

Figure 4.5: An image segmentation example with mean shift.

other. Considering this interdependence, these local dependencies translate to a global inter-dependency of the graph of labels. Even with a Markovian property, which says the label at a pixel only depends on the labels of its neighbors, there is a chain of dependence in the graph. Consider the graph representation of Figure 4.6, every label node x_i is connected to all other neighbor nodes because of local dependencies. Consequently, global optimization methods are needed to perform the segmentation.

This global optimization problem is called *inference on the graph* and consists of estimating the joint probability of scene labels and pixel intensities. To get these estimates, we consider that there is a dependence among the labels and their neighbors and a dependence between labels and the intensity at the pixel and the reduction after Bayes rule leads to the following:

$$p(x, y) = \prod_i \Phi(x_i, y_i) \prod_{i,j} \Psi(x_i, x_j), \tag{4.3}$$

where x represents the vector of all the labels and y is the vector of all observations (pixel inten-sities). If we estimate the joint probability we can get the posterior $p(x|y) = \frac{p(x,y)}{p(y)}$, (although $p(y)$ is not known we can consider it a normalization constant which does not affect the selec-tion of the most likely labels x). After taking the log, the product term becomes a summation as follows:

$$E(x, y) = \sum_i \Phi(x_i, y_i) + \prod_{i,j} \Psi(x_i, x_j), \tag{4.4}$$

where Φ and Ψ are called unary and pairwise potentials, respectively.

Segmentation is equivalent to maximizing probability or minimizing the energy term E, providing the most likely label set given the observation The probabilities often have a para-metric form and training requires finding those parameters given training data. Then on a new

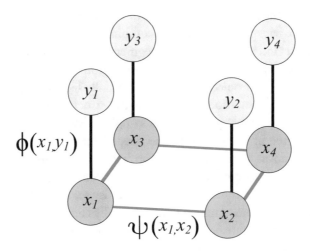

Figure 4.6: Illustration of a MRF representation for image segmentation. Pixels in the image are represented by nodes on the graph. The observation, i.e., the pixel intensity, is given by y_i and the segment labels that are unknown are given by x_i. The goal of MRF inference is to infer the latent variables x_i. Learning unary and pairwise potentials is done with training images.

image the learned unary and pairwise potentials are use to predict labels by performing graph inference to find the most likely labels given the observation. CRFs are a variation on this idea which directly models $P(x|y)$ [89, 121], but the basic idea is the same. More recent methods of CRF [118] employ efficient algorithms such as graph-cut as the inference method. Other recent methods [27] use nonparametric forms of the pairwise potential.

4.2   SEGMENTATION WITH DEEP LEARNING

Traditional segmentation methods have evolved with the advent of deep learning and convolutional neural nets. One of the major shifts is from unsupervised to supervised methods. Traditional image segmentation algorithms were typically unsupervised; that is, no knowledge of objects, surface or scenes is exploited. Instead, region delineation is based on inherent image cues such as color and color variation within the region so that like pixels are associated within contiguous regions. However, recent improvements have been made in segmentation using semantic segmentation, inspection not only of the pixel values and their relationship but also the likelihood that these pixels belong together based on some higher-level knowledge (training) about what the regions should contain. For an intuitive example, it's easier to group pixels in the tiger region (Figure 4.7) from the background, with higher-level knowledge of the expected shape and appearance of a tiger. This segmentation was generated using [235]. In fact, image segmentation based only on the pixel values are likely to fail given that the tiger stripes are intended camouflage with the the background grass. The combined algorithm of segmentation/grouping and recognition of the region is called semantic segmentation, also known as pixel-wise labeling or scene labeling. The algorithm output is segmented regions with identifying labels.

The success of CNNs for object recognition naturally led to explorations of their use for pixel-wise labeling as a segmentation. Inherent in the structure of CNNs is a loss of spatial detail caused by steps such as max-pooling and sampling. While these steps are essential for achieving a certain degree of spatial invariance needed for recognition of multiple class instances, the process removes the pixel-wise information that is needed for segmentation or pixel-based labeling. Also, classifying each pixel without constraining nearby neighbors to have similiar values (smoothness constraints) can result in noisy segmentations. Segmentation using CRFs [116, 120] uses a graph-based model that specifically constrains nearby labeling to be similar. The labeling of each pixel satisfies both similarity constraints and smoothness constraints to produce a final optimized labeling. The introduction of fully connected CRFs and efficient algorithms to handle the inference have improved segmentation accuracy [27, 116]. Semantic segmentation can be done by combining both CNNs and CRFs in order to have accurate pixel-labels and sharply delineated contiguous regions desirable in good quality segmentation (as shown in Figure 4.9). The approach of combining CNNS and CRFs has been utilized in recent work [32, 133, 235]. Alternative to CRF which yield well localized pixel-wise segmentation are domain transforms [31] using edge maps.

The Fully Convolutional Neural Network (FCN) [140, 186] is a framework that replaces the last classification layer in CNNs with a fully convolutional layer to achieve pixel-wise labeling in and end-to-end learnable network for semantic segmentation. The FCNs enable an upsampling of the deep feature maps so that the output matches the input image size and therefore can be used for a pixelwise labeling, i.e., a semantic segmentation. However, because of the downsampling inherent in the network, precise boundaries are difficult to achieve with FCN. End-to-end learning of both FCN and the CRF component was achieved by [235]. The addition of CRFs to the FCN outputs to refine boundaries has achieved significant success in recent work [30, 73].

A different approach is the method of *deconvolution networks* for segmentation [156] based on earlier work [222] on deconvolutional networks for feature learning. A deconvolutional network uses an *unpooling* strategy that that puts an activation back to its original location. Pooling layers in CNNs, such as max-pooling, remove the spatial location of the max values and this unpooling provides a way to retrieve that location. The deconvolution network trains a multilayer network to do the full upsampling and results in high accuracy boundaries for the segmented regions. Adding a CRF component further improves the results of deconvolution networks by a small amount. The approach of upsampling to achieve pixelwise labeling is also addressed in methods that learn upsampling filters [12, 30, 34].

Figure 4.7: Semantic segmentation challenging segmentation example. (Top) original image. (Center) The results were obtained using the associated demo website *Semantic Image Segmentation Live Demo*. (Bottom) Mean shift segmentation results for comparison.

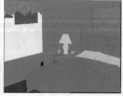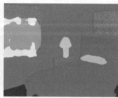

Figure 4.8: Segmentation example using EncNet [228].

Other recent directions in semantic segmentation include bottom-up region-based CNN [74, 75]. Region methods to incorporate context are also used in the pyramid-scene parsing network [232] that achieves good border localization even without CRF refinement. Region proposals are used to enable semantic segmentation in several methods [50, 74, 156].

Global cues of the scene can greatly improve the ability to perform the joint task of segmentation and semantic labeling. Knowledge of the global scene greatly increases or decreases the likelihood of certain object classes. For example, cars are likely to be near roads and boats are often near water. Utilizing global context cues have motivated several recent methods. PSPnet (pyramid scene parsing network) builds on FCN [140] and FCN with CRFs [33] and spatial pyramid pooling (SPP) [79, 87, 122]. SPP-net [87] places the spatial pyramid pooling layer as an intermediate layer between the convolutional layers and fully connected layers of a standard CNN. Motivated by the excellent performance of spatial pyramid matching in state-of-the-art large-scale object recognition, [87] incorporates SPM within SPP-net for improved object recognition and object detection. PSPnet has a pyramid processing layer inspired by SPP-net and SPM. SPM uses spatially arranged histogram for feature collection and SPP-net incorporates SPM in a CNN. PSP-net also includes a pyramid pooling layer, however, since the goal of PSP-net is segmentation instead of recognition, this layer does not use a local feature histogram. For the pyramid pooling layer, a pyramid representation is constructed from the feature map of the last convolutional layer of a CNN. A 1×1 convolution is then applied reducing the channel size to 1 for each level of the pyramid. Upsampling via interpolation gives a set of feature maps with a set size equal to the number of pyramid layers. A final convolutional layer is done to make the pixel-wise prediction resulting in a semantic segmentation.

The Context Encoding Network (EncNet) [228] provides a more explicit way to provide global context to aid segmentation. The motivation for this work is that while increasing receptive field size in a network does incorporate global information, global context can be encoded more explicitly in the network. A context encoding module as an intermediate layer CNN feature map is computed. The module computes weights that are used for context-dependent, channel-specific scaling of the original CNN feature map which is then passed to a final convolutional layer with upsampling for a pixel-wise labeling to provide a semantic segmentation. To provide global context, the context encoding module predicts object classes present in the scene using a semantic loss and the output of an Encoding Layer [223]. The encoding layer integrates

Figure 4.9: A set of examples of semantic segmentation The results were obtained using the associated demo website *Semantic Image Segmentation Live Demo* [235]. The middle and bottom row have large segmented regions that were correctly labeled as cars. The top row shows an example class that was not in the training set and was given the label "airplane" and "bird."

dictionary learning and residual encoding into a single CNN layer to capture orderless representations. The same encoding layer output is also used to estimate per-channel scale factors for the output feature maps. In this manner the channel weights depend on the context of the scene.

The progression of segmentation from classic methods to incorporate deep learning has also seen CNNs applied in spectral segmentation. For example, [148] trains CNNs to predict the similarity metric needed to define an affinity matrix. Thus we see several trends that rework classic segmentation methods with the modern deep learning methods: traditional CRFs modified with deep learning to jointly do classification and segmentation resulting in a semantic segmentation. The traditional n-cuts framework has been modified to learn the similarity measure resulting in a spectral segmentation with a more robust similarity measure. The resulting deep affinity network does segmentation and groups regions without specific labels.

A crucial component in all modern semantic segmentation methods is accurate labeling for ground truth. Since the labels are pixelwise, the number of labels is the number of image pixels. Manual, human-based labeling can be prohibitively time-consuming to generate this label set. To make the labeling process easier, *Labelme* software [174] was developed with a usable human-machine interface. However, the labeling time is still a tremendous effort. A major asset in the development of modern segmentation algorithms is the ADE20K database [17, 236] which provides extremely high-quality consistent labeling and has enabled the development of very high-quality segmentation algorithms. Recent methods that use ADE20K database for training or evaluation include [97, 132, 228, 236]. Examples of segmentation results using ADE20K and EncNet are given in Figure 4.8.

SUMMARY

In this chapter we discuss segmentation methods with an overview of classic segmentation methods. While segmentation and recognition were typically distinct algorithms in the past, the advent of deep learning simultaneous recognition and segmentation, i.e., semantic segmentation, leads to state-of-the-art results. Semantic segmentation methods include region-based methods, spectral-methods, fully connected convolutional networks FCN, CRF-based methods, and deconvolution networks.

PROBLEMS

4.1. Consider the simple graphs of Figures 4.2. Devise a slightly more complex graph with three main components to be segmented. Compute the graph Laplacian using the adjacency matrix. Compute the graph Laplacian eigenvectors using matlab command *eigs*. Show that the second eigenvector reveals the three segments.

4.2. Repeat the previous problem using an affinity matrix instead of an adjacency matrix. The affinity along edges within a group should be stronger than edges between nodes of different groups. Compute the eigenvectors and show that kmeans clustering of the second eigenvector can segment the three groups.

4.3. Visually compare mean-shift and ncuts segmentation over five real world images from the ADE20K database. In your comparison, consider memory usage, speed, and accuracy.

4.4. Visually compare the results of three CNN-based segmentation for the same five images using publicly available code. Some example networks include PSPnet [232], Encnet [228], or DeepLab [30].

4.5. Repeat the segmentation comparisons in the prior two questions using pixelwise accuracy and mean of classwise intersection-over-union (IoU).

CHAPTER 5

Texture Synthesis

Texture synthesis can be considered a test of the underlying texture representation or model. If the model is generative and sufficiently descriptive, it can create new instances of a texture class. Texture has an element of randomness, and two instances are not spatially identical. The probabilistic distribution of features along with a framework for spatial organization defines the texture class so that a particular image of a texture is an instance drawn from this model. A simple example of an application that requires texture synthesis is texture tiling, which uses texture "tiles" side-by-side to create a larger region. Using identical texture tiles is known to perform poorly because of noticeable seams at the tile boundaries. Algorithms for texture synthesis can be used to extend texture in a seamless way as demonstrated in Figure 5.1.

5.1 TRADITIONAL METHODS FOR TEXTURE SYNTHESIS

Early methods for texture synthesis were developed using multi-scale image pyramids [54, 90, 238]. The discovery in these earlier methods was that realistic texture images could be synthesized by manipulating a white noise image so that its feature statistics (characterized by either histograms or conditional histograms) matched a target. That is, the probability distribution of a particular feature is matched to the exemplar image for each level of the image pyramid [90] or the conditional probability [54] of a particular feature given the feature conditioned on the feature of the prior coarsest scale was matched. Matching these probabilities is done with histogram matching where the histograms were matched with the target at each pyramid level. The matching can be done by a standard histogram-matching algorithm based on cumulative distributions, for each pyramid level. The final image is obtained by reconstructing the image using from its pyramid decomposition. The stage of the algorithm that creates the pyramid and the feature statistics at each level is called the *analysis* stage and matching the white noise image feature statistics at each pyramid level is the *synthesis* stage. These algorithms can generate new instances of the same texture class, by using a new instance of a white noise image.

There are several classic variations on this main idea of pyramid-based representations for analysis and synthesis of texture. The pyramid synthesis approach was also extended to time-varying textures (such as flowing water and moving crowds) and texture mixtures [15]. Another extension is the replacement of standard pyramids with steerable pyramids [15, 165]. Unlike traditional Gaussian or Laplacian pyramids [163], the steerable pyramid [192] decomposes the texture image in spatial frequency bands that are also tuned for orientation. The method of [165]

Figure 5.1: Texture tiling (top) vs. texture synthesis (bottom). Seams at texture boundaries are removed because new texture of the same class is generated in a seamless manner.

also shows a matching of joint statistics, correlations of filter responses, instead of filter response histograms. Another class of algorithms uses MRF models [238] to represent the texture, and Gibbs sampling to synthesize texture. However, this method of sampling MRFs has a a long computation time for synthesis. This concept was modified by [213] which also generated texture from white noise by matching the local region to something similar in the input texture.

Another effective texture synthesis method uses exemplar texture images and varies the placement of pixels or patches. A popular and elegantly simple technique is image quilting [61, 63], as illustrated in Figure 5.2. This method does not use a multiresolution pyramid decomposition, and there is no explicit statistical representation for the texture. Unlike other traditional methods, there is no analysis stage that formulates a texture representation (e.g., statistics over multiresolution). Instead, the algorithm finds and places patches by optimizing the similarity of the patches and the surrounding regions. For many classes of natural textures,

Figure 5.2: Texture synthesis by image quilting [61, 63]. The exemplar image (left) is used to select suitable patches to create the synthesized image (right). Image credit: Wikipedia, *Texture Synthesis*. Source: http://mesh.brown.edu/dlanman/courses/en256/imagequilting.gif, Douglas Lanman.

the resulting texture synthesis is a good match to the expected appearance. However, the method relies on knowing the appropriate patch size and works best when the distribution is very regular, i.e., when the texture can be modeled as a random placement of a set of patches. The only input to this method is a single exemplar texture, so no training stage is necessary.

5.2   TEXTURE SYNTHESIS WITH DEEP LEARNING

In recent years, texture synthesis methods have progressed to incorporate deep learning and CNN architectures. The classic notions of creating specific types of images by modifying white noise input have been reformulated with CNNs. The modern methods retain the general approach of modifying white noise input to become an instance of texture by matching the texture model. For texture synthesis, the gram matrix representation [70, 71] replaces the feature histograms of prior methods and are more closely related to the second-order moments used by [165].

Layers of the network are analogous to levels of an image pyramid, in the sense that multiple resolutions are represented at different layers. In classic methods, the feature histogram at each level are the histograms pixel values of a Laplacian or steerable pyramid. For texton representations [47, 129], a filter bank is applied to the images, the output of this filter bank is clustered as a texton, and the texton histograms are the texture representation (see Chapter 2). Texture synthesis with CNNs [70] uses the cross correlation between the set of filter outputs over the entire image to create a type of gram matrix. That is, from a set of filter responses $F \in \mathbf{R}^{N \times M}$ where N is the number of filters and M are the pixel coordinates after vectorizing the image, the gram matrix G for that layer is given by $FF^T \in \mathbf{R}^{N \times N}$. Unlike the histogram representation which considers the distribution of values, of filter outputs, the diagonal elements of G retain only the mean squared values of the filter responses.

Matching the synthesized output to the input representation is done layer-by-layer, in a manner that differs from traditional methods. Instead of using a deterministic algorithm to match the histograms at each layer such as histogram matching in [90], the matching is approached as an optimization problem. In the classic pyramid methods, fixed filters are used. The image is modified at each layer so that its statistics match at that layer. The processing at each layer is independent, so there is no sense of optimizing the image as a whole. For CNN methods, the filters at each layer are learned, not fixed. The filters are learned within the end-to-end optimization using a cost function so that the gram matrix at each layer, will match. The gradient descent algorithm modifies the pixel values of the original image $i_c = i_{c-1} - \alpha \frac{\partial L}{\partial i}$, where i_c is the image at the current iteration. The derivative of the loss function L with respect to the input image pixels i can be computed via backpropagation using the expression for the derivative of the loss function with respect to each layer input as in [70]. In this optimization approach, the network is learned (i.e., the nonlinear filters at each layer) and the input image is modified (using stochastic gradient descent) until the feature representation (gram matrix) matches sufficiently well at each layer.

The drawback is that this optimization needs to be done for every new texture image, which is a relatively slow process. The optimization-based method uses a CNN to describe the texture and iteratively changes the pixels of the image until its description matches the target description. Another approach is a feed-forward method [205] that uses generative adversarial networks (GAN) [78, 166], as illustrated in Figure 5.3. The GANs have two components, a generator network that starts with white noise input and generates an image, and a discriminator which decides whether the image is real or fake [78]. The discriminator is trained by an optimization that maximizes the probability of correct labels over the training data (real) and samples from the generator network (fake). The generator network is trained at the same time to minimize the probability of the discriminator being able to tell the real data from the generated data. In game theory, this is a two-player minimax game. The discriminator and generator networks can be multilayer perceptrons and then the entire GAN can be trained using backpropagation. Using principles of game theory, training the GANs lead to new images that "match" the input and are realistic new instances. Of critical importance is that texture synthesis using a GAN network is now "feed-forward," i.e., generation required evaluation of the network, not training. The training is done in a prior stage, using multiple texture exemplars. For the generation, an instance of texture and white noise is provided as input and the GAN matches the texture instance in class (and feature statistics), without the need for optimization and SGD (stochastic gradient descent). This feed-forward approach is significantly faster (100×). A disadvantage of the GAN approach to texture synthesis is that a new network must be trained for every type of texture synthesized. Recent works [29, 95, 96, 224] have addressed this problem with variations on feed-forward networks.

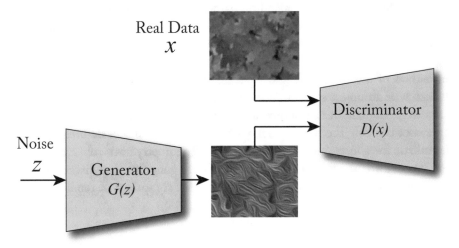

Figure 5.3: Generative Adversarial Networks (GANs) used for texture synthesis. The GANs have two components: a generator network that starts with white noise input and generates an image, and a discriminator which decides whether the image is real or fake.

Improved texture networks [204] incorporate the following enhancements to the original texture network. First, the training of the feed-forward network is done on a set of texture images uniformly sampled from the texture representation for each class. The authors discuss how optimization methods [70] can be considered a variation of classic texture synthesis [165] that generates an image by sampling from the collection of all images that have a sufficient match to the characteristic texture statistics. For [70], these statistics are the gram-matrix computed on a CNN. However, the optimization does not ensure a uniform sampling over the ensemble of images. Using a Julesz generator network [204] improves the diversity of feed forward networks by learning a generator network that better samples the collection of textures that belong to the class.

The *Markovian Generative Adversarial Network (MGAN)* [131] also generates texture with GANs but uses a patch-based approach. Statistics of patches and relationships between neighboring patches are used for the texture representation. The method uses a feed-forward network and generates textures at least 500× faster than prior feed-forward networks for texture synthesis. The disadvantage of this approach is that the network must be precomputed for each texture type, i.e., training must take place for each texture class.

The results with GANs have been very impressive beyond texture synthesis as well. The representations allow subtractions of parts and context in a way that was not previously possible. For example, in [166] an image of "man with glasses" undergoes the following transformation within the GAN representation: subtract "man" from "man with glasses" add "woman" and get images of "women with glasses." No pixel-level subtraction or addition would lead to anything meaningful without precise alignment and additional processing. However, GAN-based representation enables the subtraction by encoding parts in a direct way in hierarchical latent space. GANs have also been used to generate images from text descriptions, to manipulate objects in an interactive editor and to translate simple human modifications into new and realistic objects [237].

The method of *Texture GANs* [218] has generated images of textured objects with the input of a sketch of an object such as shoes, purse or jacket and a patch of texture analogous to a fabric swatch. The output is a photorealistic image of the textured object with the texture choice under user control. The texture GAN handles the boundaries defined by the sketch as well as the realistic foreshortening around the expected geometry of the object, although no 3D information is provided. The network, comprised of both generator and discriminator, learns to generate realistic appearance by using a large training set comprised of retail images depicting shoes, handbags, and clothes.

SUMMARY

In this chapter we have discussed the texture synthesis methods with an overview of classic approaches that focused on matching a texture representation based on pyramids or on nonparametric sampling. Recent CNN-based methods of texture synthesis have emerged and generative adversarial networks show significant advances. The current approaches of texture synthesis integrate scene context as well, so that textures are generated in the context of a more complex scene.

PROBLEMS

5.1.   Implement and test the Heeger–Bergen method [90] for texture synthesis. Identify both successful texture synthesis classes and challenge cases where the algorithm fails.

5.2.   Repeat the texture synthesis using feed-forward texture networks [205] or a generative adversarial networks [78]. Comment on the performance of the texture networks compared to the pyramid representation. Identify three reasons for the difference.

5.3.   Hypothesize a new match measure for a feed-forward texture network instead of the gram matrix. Explain the reasons for your selection.

CHAPTER 6

Texture Style Transfer

6.1 TRADITIONAL METHODS OF STYLE TRANSFER

Style transfer is a framework that transfers the style of one image (that often includes patterns and textures) onto a second image while retaining the semantic content of that second image. When we consider the *prediction and synthesis* requirement for a computational texture representation, as discussed in Chapter 1, texture transfer can be viewed as a type of synthesis where the goal is a representation that can separate and then transfer content and texture (style). The notion of separating the content from the style of images has origins in bilinear models [198] that separate content and style for text characters where the content is the character shape but the style is how the character is drawn or written. For images, the style is often the artistic style of a painted scene or some natural texture within a scene (e.g., stone, brick, foliage). The texture transfer retains the shape of the object in the image, but uses the texture of the style image. The result is either an object with a new texture or an object painted with a specified artistic style. The underlying representations for texture transfer algorithms often are similar to those of texture synthesis algorithms. For example, texture quilting can be used for both synthesis and texture transfer [62]. Image analogies is a related method that transfers a textural style to a content image [91] by using a multiscale matching of patches within a Gaussian pyramid. Additional traditional approaches to texture transfer include natural texture synthesis [10] which enables user-specified content via a user-drawn content sketch, example-based cosmetic transfer [199] which transfers cosmetic application to faces via style transfer, and hole-filling with Patch Match [16].

6.2 TEXTURE STYLE TRANSFER WITH DEEP LEARNING

Recent texture style transfer replaces feature histograms at pyramid levels with a gram-matrix representation using multilayer neural networks. Gatys et al. [70, 71] first used a pre-trained CNN as a descriptive representation of image statistics and provides an explicit representation that separates image style and content information. This method is *optimization-based* because the new texture image is generated by applying gradient descent that manipulates a white noise image to match the gram-matrix representation of the target image. Recent work [102, 205] trains a feed-forward generative network to approximate the optimization process for style transfer leading to a much faster run time. For these approaches a separate network is trained for each different style. Methods for multi-style transfer have now been developed so that one network can be used for multiple styles. Chen et al. [29] use mid-level convolutional filters for each style and Zhang et al. [224] introduce MSG-net with an end-to-end learnable layer that provides multi-style generation from a single network. MSG-net explicitly matches the feature statistics at multiple scales in order to retain the performance of optimization-based methods and achieve the speed of feed-forward networks. It uses a siamese network that comprises a co-match layer to match feature statistics of the style image to the original image using gram-matrix matching within a feed-forward network. This network enables brush-size control by resizing the style image.

Many style transfer methods transfer the style of artistic paintings and deep networks seem to capture this type of style well. Interestingly, when inverting deep representations [147] of photographs that are not paintings, the result has an artistic painting appearance. For style transfer, when the original image and target style image are not paintings, the transfer algorithm is more challenging. When transferring styles between photographs, a style reminscent of paintings appears in the output, even if the input and target images are photographs with no painting style. The method of *Deep Photo Style Transfer* [142] addresses this problem with a method that uses a locally affine constraint in colorspace to avoid distortions.

6.3   FACE STYLE TRANSFER

Human faces are a particularly interesting pattern in images, and the human brain is hardwired to detect/find and recognize faces [107]. Transferring texture or style in human face images enables interesting and useful digital effects. For the application of painting style transfer to head portraits, [185] builds a CNN-based approach that enforces spatial constraints in the form of local color distributions. This network is not tuned to a particular style, but expects an input example of a painting-type style. Photo-style transfer with deep networks enables the generation of portrait style images from ordinary photographs [189]. Photo-realistic facial texture transfer with *FaceTex* [109] enables automatic generation of synthetically aged and de-aged faces as illustrated in the results of Figure 6.3. Deep feature interpolation [206] uses linear interpolation of features from pre-trained CNNs with excellent results in creating effects of aging, de-aging, facial hair, and glasses.

PROBLEMS

6.1. Using a publicly available implementation of style transfer, apply the methods to three examples of input images and target images. The implementation for MSG-net can be found at https://github.com/zhanghang1989/MSG-Net. What type of image pairs does the method work best for? What are the limitations?

6.2. Automatic face appearance modification. Using five face images, use deep feature interpolation to change the age, add facial hair and add glasses using the code at: https://github.com/paulu/deepfeatinterp.

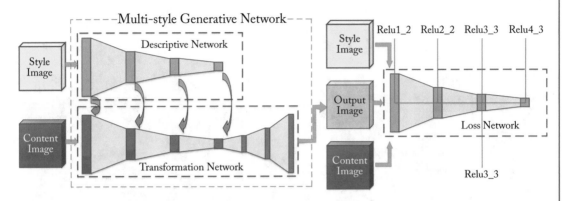

Figure 6.1: An overview of MSG-Net (Multi-style Generative Network) [224]. A pre-trained loss network provides the supervision of MSG-Net learning by minimizing the content and style differences with the targets. Figure from [224].

Figure 6.2: Examples of texture style transfer. From Left to Right: original image, optimization-based method [71], feed-forward method [102], MSG-net [224]. The transformation network as part of the generator explicitly matches the features statistics captured by a descriptive network of the style targets. A pre-trained loss network provides the supervision of MSG-net learning by minimizing the content and style differences with the targets. Figure from [224].

| Input 1 (I_1) | Input 2 (I_2) | Style:I_1, Content:I_2 | Style:I_2, Content:I_1 |

Figure 6.3: From [109], examples of face texture style transfer. Identity-preserving Facial Texture Transfer (FaceTex). The textural details are transferred from style image to content image while preserving its identity. FaceTex outperforms existing methods perceptually as well as quantitatively. Column 3 uses input 1 as the style image and input 2 as the content. Column 4 uses input 1 as the content image and input 2 as the style image. Input photos: Martin Scheoller/Art+Commerce.

CHAPTER 7

Return of the Pyramids

7.1 ADVANTAGES OF PYRAMID METHODS

Traditional methods in computer vision use pyramid representations extensively for representing features. Methods described as multiscale, coarse-to-fine, hierarchical, or multiresolution typically employ a pyramid representation. Laplacian pyramids and Gaussian pyramids [163] are easy to compute and provide speed up for algorithms. Bandpass decompositions enabled representations of features that separated image content per spatial frequency band, an approach particularly suitable for representing textures. Additionally, the lower spatial frequency content in coarser levels of the pyramid enable accurate representation of image gradients using discrete approximation of derivatives. (Image gradients are often approximated by a difference filter that only approximates a gradient calculation and is particularly inaccurate for high-frequency image content.)

With the advent of deep learning, multiple layers seemed to initially replace pyramids as a multiscale decomposition. Deep learning networks incorporate downsampling so that the effective resolution of the upper layers are lower than the original image and convolutions in upper layers encompass more global information while convolution on lower layers have local information. However, in recent years, research paths show a *return of the pyramids* where traditional Laplacian and Gaussian pyramids are taking their place as components within larger networks. The term *pyramid network* is often used to describe this hybrid entity where convolutions with fixed filters in a coarse-to-fine framework are present in the network and not tuned according to training data. The value of the pyramid representation with fixed filters is apparent in their convenient off-the-shelf use without requiring further optimization.

Examples of pyramid networks include *Feature Pyramid Networks* [59, 135, 164] used for object detection. The idea in these pyramid networks is that multiple levels of the pyramid are processed to compute feature maps. One method [164] uses a bottom-up/top-down approach where predictions are made at the finest level, while [135] also uses a top-down pyramid components but with independent predictions at each level. A strong motivation for using pyramids within the CNN architecture is the recent success of image classification methods. Spatial pyramid pooling [86] is a version of spatial pyramid matching [122] which pools feature in bins. The spatial extent of each bin is proportional to the image size so that the output of a spatial pyramid pooling is fixed even for arbitrary input image sizes. The binning is done using a pyramid constructed from the feature maps. This spatial pyramid pooling layer ports spatial pyramid matching into the CNN and uses fixed filters to accomplish pyramid construction. For image segmentation, recent methods for semantic segmentation incorporate pyramids in the deep architecture including PSPnet [231] and Laplacian pyramid-based semantic segmentation [73]. The advantage is the upsampling and reconstruction that pyramid methods can easily accomplish; image reconstruction is obtained by a linear combination of multiple upsampled levels. Upsampling in these traditional pyramids is done by zero-insertion folllowed by convolution with the Gaussian filter to interpolate samples. In the application of photo-editing, fast local Laplacian filters [11] achieves image-level control without introducing obvious artifacts, demonstrating that photo-realistic operations in CNNs are well supported by local Laplacian filters within their architecture. Interestingly, the fusion of image pyramids and CNNs come in two varieties. In one set of methods, the CNN architecture is retained and the pyramid processing is a component or layer within the traditional network. However, [56] uses a different approach where the deep learning architecture (in this case a GAN) is used as a component in a traditional coarse-to-fine pyramid framework. At the coarsest scale, white noise is used as a seed to generate the coarsest level l of the pyramid using a GAN, then this generated image is upsampled to move to the next finest level $l - 1$ where the process is repeated and a new GAN is used to generate the updated image at level $l - 1$. These steps repeat again until the finest level image is generated.

This similarity in the application and intuition of pyramids and multilayer deep networks indicates that future work will continue exploration of hybrid methods that use both fixed and learned filters.

CHAPTER 8

Open Issues in Understanding Visual Patterns

8.1 DISCOVERING UNKNOWN PATTERNS

Most of the recent successes in representing visual patterns using deep learning are based on supervised methods that rely on known class labels. When we know what we are looking for, such as the class label of a particular object, and when we have examples of that class (preferably millions of examples), optimization of a deep model such as a convolutional network provides a powerful representation. However, consider the case when the task at hand requires mining data without knowing what to look for. Perhaps some of the most interesting patterns are those that cannot be predicted before-hand. For instance, examples may include a surprising weather pattern, stock-market pattern, gene structure [92], traffic pattern, cybercrimes, or a social networking pattern such as emails within an organization [173]. When the patterns are not known a priori, the goal is pattern discovery [212] which is significantly more challenging than recognition.

8.2 DETECTING SUBTLE CHANGE

In real applications, object and surface appearance is more complex than the metrics of size, shape, color, and label. Texture properties are fundamentally more challenging and require computational models that will account for inherent variations that do not indicate real change. Recent deep learning models have enabled learning of powerful invariance within object models, e.g., different types of dogs may still be labeled as "dog." Texture requires similar intra-class invariance, but also typically uses orderless representations that rely less on spatial ordering of features.

Detecting change in patterns is particularly important and sometimes elusive, especially for very small subtle changes. For example, consider a potential question in quantitative dermatology: *Is the appearance of psoriasis changed by one week of an expensive treatment?* If quantification of 3% change can be made, motivation for continuation to 8 weeks is readily given. The problem of quantifying subtle changes in appearance typically relies on a human expert that can detect and interpret the relevant patterns. This problem is at the core of many real-world tasks such as structural inspection (to asses the condition of steel and concrete); manufacturing quality control (to assess the surface texture or consumer items such from textiles to steel); advanced automobiles (to detect black ice and other hazardous road surfaces); quantitative dermatology (to automatically monitor skin change); and advanced agriculture (to monitor plant condition in modern vertical farms). While automated methods in computer vision have been refined and deployed, the success remains primarily in automated prediction of semantic labels (what the object is) and determining 3D structure.

The challenge is to determine whether the appearance has changed, but color appearance measurements are susceptible to lighting and camera sensitivity. Texture changes are even harder to detect because pixel-by-pixel comparison cannot be made. Change detection must be based on change of a computational representation. An additional challenge is determining what change is meaningful. The representations, especially those based on complex neural networks can possibly have perturbed numeric values in the representation, but still represent the same textured regions. Therefore, an outstanding problem is a sensitivity analysis of the texture representation. The goal is a representation where change in numeric values indicate actual changes in texture appearance.

8.3   PERCEPTUAL METRICS

In considering change detection, it is also natural to consider how change is perceived. If the human is the end-user (such as applications in e-commerce, design, and general graphics), comparison of textures needs a metric that is consistent with human perception. Comparison of two textures to see how they match should consider how well they match to the human. Studies of texture perception develop similarity metrics that are useful for image search and other applications [239]. These perceptual quality metrics can also be useful in evaluatiing texture synthesis algorithms. While perceptual metrics have been proposed [60], extensive studies of human perception compared with the computational metric is an area of open work. The concept of *texture metamers* is to determine why two texture regions may be perceived as the same texture class is an interesting and open topic of investigation.

CHAPTER 9

Applications for Texture and Patterns

In this chapter we consider the question: *Why study texture?* There are countless applications for analyzing and modeling visual patterns. We discuss specific examples covering industrial, medical, scientific, and consumer applications.

9.1 MEDICAL IMAGING AND QUANTITATIVE DERMATOLOGY

Internal imaging using CT and MRI has received significant attention in recent years. A great advance in the field was development of computational algorithms to precisely align multiple images taken over time. Alignment has enabled image-guided surgery [117, 128], replacing the need for stereotactic frames [143] that are physically attached to a patient's skull prior to brain surgery. The exact position of a tumor as identified in pre-operative images can be obtained in the operating room during surgery. Computational alignment has also enabled change detection since aligned and calibrated digital images can be subtracted pixel-by-pixel to highlight even small changes.

In medical diagnosis, detecting and delineating tumor regions has received significant attention. However, more subtle detection is based on the texture within a CT, MRI, PET, or some other medical image. Specific areas of medical evaluation that routinely rely on texture or patterns include the detection and evaluation of a brain tumor [99], liver lesions [68, 76, 155], lung disease [67, 69, 152], and skin cancer [64].

Similar advances in medical imaging are happening in dermatology [46, 49, 64, 144, 154]. Clinical dermatology has not yet benefited from the ability to standardize images in a computationally meaningful way, but the need clearly exists. Consider the impact of meaningful numbers representing skin change. By recording and plotting skin change in response to a treatment, the outcome could be predicted earlier than with visual assessment. Quantitative comparisons could also be made between different treatments. Research in this area will open up a new field of quantitatively characterizing skin appearance for treatment, diagnosis, and drug development. In modeling texture, the change in the computational texture representation (e.g., model coefficients) can indicate change in a quantifiable manner. This change detection is an example of *gradient computation* in the texture model requirements, as outlined in Chapter 1.

9.2 TEXTURE MATCHING IN INDUSTRY

In developing replacement materials and paints for repairs and renovations, color matching is a well-known issue. Texture matching has received much less attention, but is equally important. Choosing the correct wood, tile, carpet, or stone requires that the pattens at the boundaries match. In most cases, these matches are currently done manually by visual inspection [143] but could be automated with sufficiently rich texture models.

Manufacturing quality control is another application domain for texture/pattern quantiative models. For example, due to the manufacturing or polishing process, sheet metal may exhibit an "orange peel" effect which gives an undesirable texture [126, 153, 179, 216]. To quantify quality control, the characteristics of such texture can be modeled to optimize the manufacturing processes.

For most applications, it is difficult to have an absolute metric of the quality of a texture. Instead, texture evaluation should be a textural comparison, a relative measure of appearance compared to a gold standard or to a prior time interval. Computer vision work on relative attributes [159] follow this theme and create a representation based on similarity. For material, perceptual attributes [182] also enable quantitative similarity based on perception of surface attributes.

9.3 E-COMMERCE

For e-commerce applications, conveying texture is important as an aesthetic. Low-resolution imagery within e-commerce is fast and efficient; however, texture is lost or corrupted by jpeg compression (see Figure 9.1). Recent methods using dictionary learning can remove some of these compression artifacts [28]. The texture information is important for aesthetic evaluation of a material. Conveying high-resolution details using texture synthesis (as discussed in Chapter 5) provides a method of recreating texture on the client side.

Similar to e-commerce, architectural details on built structures provide a visual pattern that is useful for aesthetics and can help in recognition. In this application, one considers the texture of brick, windows, facades, and marble and considers recognition for analyzing existing architecture and for digital storage of this object. Pattern recognition can assist object description (storing images under the type of architectural detail), clustering similar facade styles, brick patterns, stone patterns, wood patterns, and stained glass. Architectural styles can be categorized and cataloged with visual patterns.

9.4 TEXTURED SOLAR PANELS

Another specific application domain is in the area of creating physical textures for a specific industrial purpose. For example, patterns in solar panels improve light absorption. Structural textures with light-trapping properties can be etched on silicon, such as multiscale textures [195, 200], honeycomb texture [134, 233], and pyramidal array [211]. Arbitrary relief

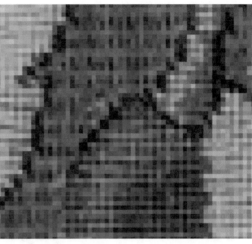

Figure 9.1: (Left) Original photograph of textile. (Right) Enlarged area showing jpeg compression artifacts that corrupts visual appearance and impedes applications where conveying realistic appearance is essential. (Photo Metropolitan Museum of Art, Open Access, Accession Number:64.101.1305, 17th century. Credit Line: Gift of Irwin Untermyer, 1964.)

textures are potentially achievable with 3D printing [58]. The intuition behind this idea is that simple, smooth, shiny surfaces reflect light well and therefore lose solar energy. An etched surface texture creates a rough surface that causes light scattering or light-trapping. In this manner, more light can be absorbed by the panel resulting in a higher efficiency rating.

9.5 ROAD ANALYSIS FOR AUTOMATED DRIVING

Automated driving requires interpretation of the road and surroundings. At first glance, the road surface may be considered simple as typical asphalt with white or yellow predictable lane markings. However, in the real world, road appearance has numerous surprises and the more typical road is shown in Figure 9.2 where the wear of snow, ice, and plows create a textured region that must be interpreted as lane markings. Worn lane marking are presenting a serious problem to the implementation of self-driving cars [177]. Modeling appearance in terms of texture can account for realistic and natural variations. Also relevant to quickly parsing road scenes is ignoring regions that are not relevant to the driving task, such as the wooded regions beyond the road. The details of the wooded region are not needed, however the semantic region label is useful for indicating a potential for deer crossing the road.

Figure 9.2: Challenging road appearance is far different from ideal conditions with a dark road and clear, white, retroreflective lines. Because of worn lane markings, road repair, and other road conditions, visual patterns are complex and models are needed for correct interpretation in automated driving tasks.

CHAPTER 10

Tools for Mining Patterns: Cloud Services and Software Libraries

Visual data accessible to data scientists has been growing exponentially over the last decade. Sources of visual data include surveillance camera live video feeds, videos uploaded to YouTube, ImageNet, and archived digital photographs of art and textures. For example, the open access at the Metropolitan Museum of Art (`metmuseum.org/openaccess`) provides over 375,000 digital photographs of artwork in the collection. Satellite imagery is available from the National Weather service and National Oceanic and Atmospheric Administration (`www.weather.gov`) including infrared, visible and water vapor. Google earth and street view provides visual imagery at multiple scales from satellite to street level. To specifically support automated driving, recent datasets such as BDD-Nexar [146], KITTI [72], Cityscapes [41], and Oxford RobotCar Dataset [145] have detailed images and/or maps of local roads.

The goal of mining patterns is the transformation *from data to knowledge* that obtains useful information from visual or non-visual data. An infamous example is the Enron email dataset that was mined to determine social and leadership hierarchy [57, 111, 187].

The computational challenge of mining patterns in visual data is often more difficult than non-visual data since the size of visual imagery is so vast. For example, with 5 letters per word and approximately 200 words per email is approximately 1 K (kilobyte) of memory. A standard size color image requires 3000 times more memory than an email (using an image of 1280 × 720 that is approximately 3 MB (megabyte). Videos obtained at a frame rate of 30 frames per second (fps) and are typically compressed. For example, a 40 minute video with compression rate of 5 Mbps (megabits per second) requires 1.5 GB (gigabyte) to store. Consider a mere 1,000 videos in the database and the size is already in the terabyte range. Obtaining and maintaining access to suitable computational resources is a crucial element of visual data mining. The medium-sized lab with desktop PCs are limited in their ability to implement and run algorithms that require processing large data sets (e.g., as in deep learning).

In this chapter we discuss some of the tools and resources that are widely available to achieve sufficient computational power for mining visual patterns. Cloud-based computing and open-source software have created means of sharing and accessing resources to greatly expand the computing capacity of small- and medium-sized labs.

10.1   SOFTWARE LIBRARIES

Software libraries that enable rapid implementation of neural networks have been developed and continue to evolve. Some prominent examples include Torch, Pytorch, Theanos, Tensorflow, Keras, and Caffe. A major advantage of using libraries is the automatic computation of gradients after setting up layers in a standard manner. For example, these libraries have automatic differentiation package (e.g., Torch.autograd) that automatically differentiates arbitrary scale-valued functions. For complex architectures and loss functions, this greatly simplifies code writing. The other convenience of these libraries is fast switching between CPU and GPU implementations. Each library was developed in a different research group in either industry or academia or both. Keras is a library written on top of a base library such as Theano or Tensorflow. The libaries use different programming languages, e.g., Torch(Lua), Pytorch(Python), Theanos(Python), Tensorflow(C++,Python), Keras(Python), and Caffe(C++). As of this writing, a comparison chart of deep learning libraries is available.[1]

10.2   CLOUD SERVICES

General cloud services allow users to use the cloud for computation or for storage. This has radically changed computing in research labs. The individual machines neither store nor process the datasets but rather act as a controlling unit to direct what computation is done on the cloud on data stored on the cloud. Examples of popular cloud services include Amazon Web Services (AWS), Google Cloud Platform (GCP), and Microsoft Azure. These services are for-fee services, however, and large computations and datasets can be expensive.

Between the cloud services and the end-user, resources specific to computer vision and machine learning have been developed. CloudCV [4] is a pioneering system for distributed computer vision algorithms on the cloud. CloudCV is composed of virtual machines running on AWS. Distributed storage is handled by Hadoop Distributed File System (HDFS) which was developed to run on low-cost commodity hardware. CloudCV allows a user to upload an algorithm and an image list and the service distributes the computation of applying the algorithm each image in parallel and returns results in real time. The image list may be from standard computer vision datasets that are preloaded on CloudCV. Similarly, the algorithms can be user-defined or from a standard collection of algorithms. If standard features of images from standard datasets are used, those features may be uploaded from distributed storage on CloudCV. In order to use services such as CloudCV, APIs have been developed by the web service provider in order to facilitate application development with their services. For example, the CloudCV Python API uses a PCloudCV class to access algorithms such as classification and feature extraction using deep CNNs and gigapixel image stitching,

The major cloud services such as Amazon, Google, and Microsoft have developed computer vision APIs for developing CV applications with their cloud services. Google Cloud Vision

---

[1]https://en.wikipedia.org/wiki/Comparison_of_deep_learning_software

is an API that utilizes Google Cloud Platform to execute computer vision algorithms such as face detection and text recognition. Amazon Rekognition API enables access to computer vision algorithms using AWS for object and face recognition, age estimation, face similarity, and appropriate content monitoring. Microsoft Computer Vision API uses Microsoft Azure and also has a suite of computer vision algorithms including recognition, handwritten text transcription, thumbnail generation, and description generation. Clarifai is a start-up that has emerged as a leader in cloud-based computer vision APIs. IBM also has visual recognition as part of their cloud-based services to "quickly and accurately tag, classify and train visual content using machine learning."[2]

Visual pattern assessment can be used by automated driving, robotic systems, and internet of things for real time analysis of appearance. Companies and labs are leveraging the power of cloud services with the associated computer vision APIs to enhance their business and research function. For example, Box uses Google Cloud Vision so that text on images is recognized and included as metadata.[3] Robotics can benefit from visual pattern analysis by storing to and accessing large shared image repositories [93, 110]. Robotics grasping uses visual patterns mined from massive databases to better plan a robust grasping sequence [108, 130]. Geo-localization for robotic systems allows robots to localize themselves on world-wide coordinates using visual patterns observable from on-board camera systems [14, 176, 221]. These systems use shared visual databases such as Google StreetView that recognize the current system position.

---

[2]https://www.ibm.com/watson/services/visual-recognition/
[3]www.box.com

APPENDIX A

A Concise Description of Deep Learning

Recently, deep learning has been applied to the problem of texture modeling in several interesting ways. In this chapter, we first provide a brief tutorial on deep learning. This tutorial provides a very basic introduction meant to remove many of the jargon terms for a straightforward and simplified description for accessibility to a wide range of beginner readers. (Readers familiar with deep learning should skip this chapter.) Most relevant here is the application of deep learning to texture recognition, segmentation, and synthesis.

The terms *deep learning* and *convolutional neural nets* give the connotation of an extremely complicated algorithmic framework. However, we can describe deep learning in a fairly simple way. For the purposes of this discussion, we consider deep learning for the problem of object recognition from images. Essentially, deep learning is finding a function that has an input x and an output y in a straightforward function $y = f(x)$. However, x is an image, not a scalar and the function $f(x)$ returns a numeric value that indicates the class (e.g., dog = 1, cat = 2, and so on). If the process has worked correctly, $f(x) = 1$ whenever a dog image is provided as the input x. It is extremely challenging to find this function. The output must take into account images of any breed of dog, from any angle, under any illumination condition, within any scene. It almost seems impossible to construct such a function, yet clearly the human brain is an existence proof that such computation can be done (albeit with substantial training).

SVM as a Linear Classifier As a preface for understanding deep learning, it is helpful to look at two basic classification algorithms that find functions that can also be used as classifiers: support vector machines (SVM) and logistic regression. Consider the two-class SVM case where the input is a $n \times 1$ feature vector x containing some information or features of the data and the output of $f(x)$ should indicate the predicted class. Suppose, for example, we want to build a classifier to tell apples from tomatoes and we have some labeled data (real) which shows the mean and variance of a the red color channel (from an RGB camera) using a training set comprised of known image patches from each class. Figure A.1 shows the training data where each point is an apple or tomato indicated by "*" or "o". We wish to find a function so that for new data (not in the training set) $f(x)$ will provide the answer to the tomato vs. apple classification. Basic SVM separates data by a line (in 2D) or a plane (in 3D) or a hyperplane in higher dimensions.

Specifically,

$$f(x) = a^T x + b \tag{A.1}$$

and the sign of $f(x)$ indicates the class. From Figure A.1, we can see that the training data is separated by drawing a line optimally spaced between the two groups. The problem of fitting this line is well understood and given training data, one can easily find the best line that separate the data via a convex optimization problem (see, for example, Exercise A.4). The SVM algorithm finds the parameters of the best line. Notice that the hyperplane is a linear combination of the data $a^T x$ plus an offset b. The optimization finds the best parameters a and b according to the training data. For an SVM, this problem is convex and off-the-shelf iterative solvers will converge to a global optimal solution.

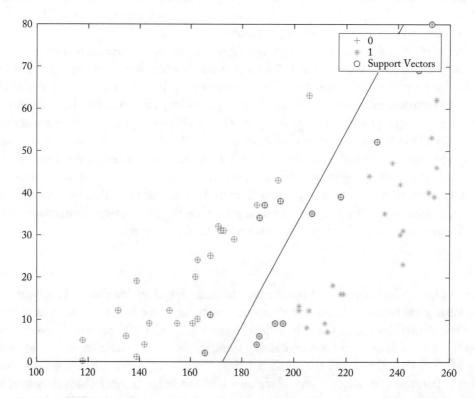

Figure A.1: An SVM classifier to classify tomato vs. apple. The training data are the mean and variance of 10×10 patches of images of known class (apple "*" or tomato "+"). The best SVM separator is shown by the line.

Logistic Regression as a Classifier   Now consider another two classifiers that fits training data to the nonlinear logistic function given by

$$f(x) = \frac{\exp(c^T x + d)}{1 + \exp(c^T x + d)}. \tag{A.2}$$

Here, $f(x)$ indicates the probability that the input feature vector $x \in \mathbf{R}^n$ is from the first class. Then, $1 - f(x)$ is the probability that the input is from the second class. Consider the same problem of identifying whether the image is the apple or a tomato based on the mean and variance of a the red color channel (from an RGB camera) using a training set. Here we want to fit a logistic function that returns "0" for apple and "1" for tomato. The logistic function is like a threshold function and has a two main parameters $a \in \mathbf{R}^n$ and $b \in \mathbf{R}$. These parameters determine the smoothness or the width of the transition region and the location of the transition. Finding the parameters of the logistic function is a convex optimization problem that can be solved with well-established methods.

Logistic Regression and SVM are two examples of classifiers, but in modern machine learning these are relatively simple methods that lack the sophistication to deal with challenging problems in real-world pattern recognition. However, the classifiers illustrate the building blocks of deep learning: weighted sums and nonlinear activation functions. The SVM takes a weighted sum of the inputs (i.e., $a^T x$) and the best weights a are learned by the training data. The logistic regression function is a nonlinear, thresholding-type function. The term activation function is used to describe this function because it switches from off "0" to on "1" in a manner determined by its parameters, as shown in Figure A.2. These weighted sums and nonlinear activation functions are the building blocks of deep learning.

A.1   MULTILAYER PERCEPTRON

Consider a simple neural net called the perceptron [171]. We see from Figure A.5 that the perceptron takes a linear sum of the input (similar to the hyperplane functions in SVM) and includes a nonlinear function (similar to the logistic function). Using a perceptron requires finding the parameters of the linear combination and the parameters for the nonlinear function. The perceptron is simply a function of the input $f(x) = y$ where y is the prediction label. The difference is that $f(x)$ is now be composed of two steps, $f(x) = f1(f2(x))$, where $f1$ is the nonlinear function and $f2$ is the linear combination of the inputs x. The next step in moving toward an understanding of deep learning is to consider the multilayer perceptron. Following [22], the multilayer perceptron looks as shown in Figure A.6. For images, the nodes represent pixels in the image. The equations are as follows:

$$Z_m = S(a_m^T X + b_m) \qquad m = 1, \dots, M \tag{A.3}$$

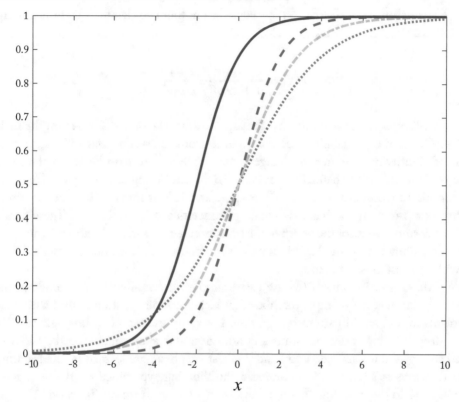

Figure A.2: The logistic function for acting on $x \in \mathbf{R}$ as $f(x) = \frac{\exp(c^T x + d)}{1 + \exp(c^T x + d)}$ for different parameter values c and d. For illustration purposes, c and x are scalars but in a typical problem, c and x can be a high dimensional vectors. Choice of c affects the sharpness of the transition region and d shifts the transition region.

with S as the sigmoid function given by

$$S(v) = \frac{1}{1 + \exp^{-\alpha v + v_o}} \tag{A.4}$$

and $X, a_m \in \mathbf{R}^P$,

$$T_k(Z) = q_k^T Z + r \qquad k = 1, \ldots, K \tag{A.5}$$

with $Z, q_k \in \mathbf{R}^M$, and

$$p_k(X) = \frac{\exp^{T_k}}{\sum_{i=1}^{K} \exp^{T_i}}. \tag{A.6}$$

In composing several functions we see how the network (i.e., the function) is comprised of multiple layers which adds "depth" to the classifier, hence the term "deep learning." The learning

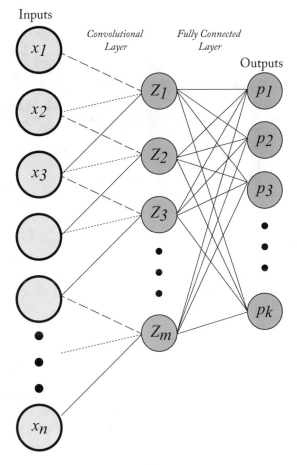

Figure A.3: A convolutional neural network has one or more convolutional layers. In a convolutional layer the nodes are connected to a local neighborhood of input nodes and weighting coefficients are shared, i.e., the local neighborhood of another node in the layer has the same input weights. In this diagram, the convolutional layer on the left illustrates the shared weights by line style, e.g., dashed edge style represents the same weight.

part is simply finding the best parameters for all the intermediate functions. In this example of multilayer perceptrons the parameters are a_m, b_m, α, v_o, q, and r.

A.2   CONVOLUTIONAL NEURAL NETWORKS

Within a layer, the nodes which compute a linear function of input data often take a particular form in modern deep learning networks. If the weights of the sum are the same for each node, i.e., the neighborhood of inputs have the same weights with respect to their position in

Figure A.4: Conceptual diagram of training for deep learning. The deep learning network is tunable (and has many parameters of knobs). During training, tune parameters until output is correct for all the training images. This tuning is done by the optimization process, often stochastic gradient descent. If the network generalizes or *learns*, the output will be correct for other input image that are not in the training set.

the neighborhood, then the operation is a convolution. Such networks are called convolutional neural nets or CNN. Additionally, the connections include neighbors in a region around each pixel, not all pixels in the image. The number of parameters are greatly reduced, making training more manageable, and the performance for recognition is high. As with any supervised classifier, the parameters are learned by optimizing the performance, e.g., recognition performance using a labeled training set where the correct class is known. Then, once the network is trained, i.e., all the parameters are estimated via optimization, the network can be used as a classifier for unknown images. That is, the network is a function for the input $f(x) = y$ where y is the output label and x are in input image pixels as shown in Figure A.7.

Convolutional Layer   Image convolutions provide a means to emphasize specific image features by using filters. This method of feature extraction has a long history in image processing and computer vision. For intuition consider the filtering of an image with three different filters as shown in Figure A.8. The original image has been convolved with a filter that blurs and computes an approximate gradient filter (both horizontal and vertical gradients are shown). The filters were chosen in this image to perform specific function. The coefficients of the blurring filter are given by a Gaussian filter and the gradient is simply a different filter that computes the difference of neighboring filters in either the horizontal or vertical direction. We can consider the output of the filtering process as a *feature map*. In Figure A.8, because there were 3 filters chosen, this is considered a *channel depth* of 3, (or Number of Channels = 3). The feature maps shown in Figure A.8 were from fixed filters. The main point in deep learning is that the

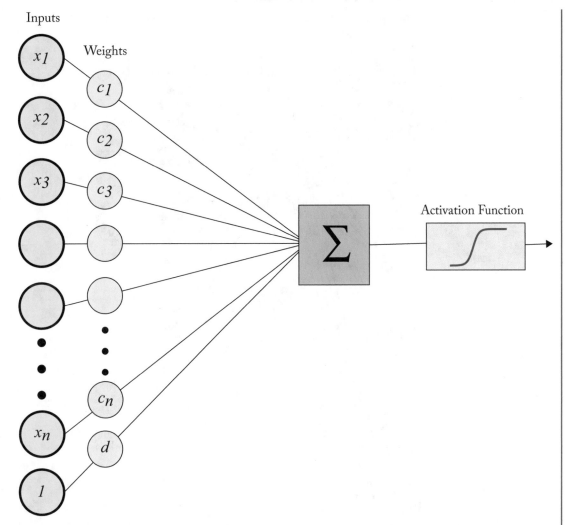

Figure A.5: The perceptron as a model of the a neuron. Computationally, the model takes a linear sum of the multiple inputs followed by a nonlinear activation function.

filter coefficients are not fixed, but rather learned in the training process. This allows important flexibility for the network to be tuned to the task at hand.

When the connections in a multilayer perceptron of Figure A.6 connect to only a local neighborhood of nodes at the previous layer and the weights for the summation are the same in each neighborhood, the operation is a convolution. When a layer is defined in this manner it is a convolutional layer. The size of the neighborhood of nodes is the size of the filter in the convolution and is referred to as the *receptive field*.

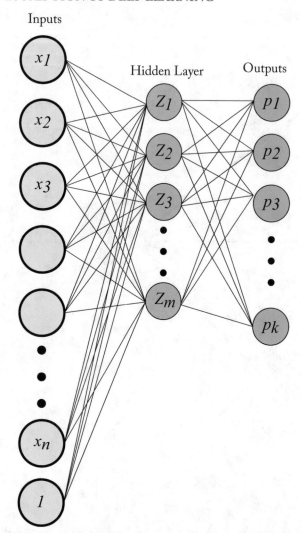

Figure A.6: The multilayer perceptron has multiple layers comprised of compositing weighted average of inputs and nonlinear functions. A single hidden layer is shown here for clarity, but multiple layers are typical. The edges between nodes represent that the input nodes are weighted and summed and a nonlinear activation function is applied (as shown explicitly in Figure A.5).

Convolutional layers have the advantage of smaller number of parameters. But fully connected layers are typically needed at the final output layers. For example, Alexnet has at its last layer a fully connected layer followed by a softmax function that provides the output probability p_i for class i.

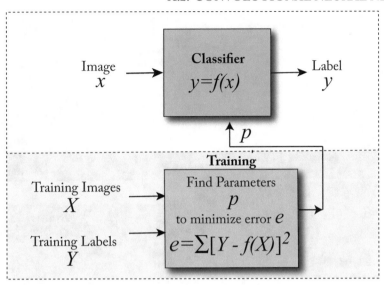

Figure A.7: Deep learning finds a function defined by $y = f(x)$ to output the class label y for the input image x. The parameters of the function f are found by minimizing the error e of the class labels over the training set. This training stage finds the optimal parameters p to define the best function f.

Pooling Layer   In CNNs subsampling is done with a pooling operation. The dimensions can be reduced by pooling operations such as max pooling (choose only the maximum in a region) or average pooling (average the local region). The pooling can be done spatially, or over the channel depth (dimension that represents different filters) or both. Also, subsampling can be done by strided convolution which essentially skips over regions of the input. For example a convolution with a stride of 2 is identical to convolving the entire image but then retaining every other pixel.

Training   Training of deep learning networks is a setting of all the coefficients (weights for the weighted sum and parameters of the nonlinear activation functions) by an optimization procedure which minimizes the loss function (also called an objective function or cost function). The loss function is simply a measure of how well the network predicts the labels of the training data. Training can be thought of conceptually as tuning a network with thousands of parameters so that the output matches the expected output (since the expected output is known in a labeled training set). A conceptual view of training deep learning networks is shown in Figure A.4. The network has many (thousands or millions) or parameters that are obtained by trying to match the output to the known input. The training procedure consists of computing a forward pass on the set of all inputs X to obtain a current prediction $\hat{Y}$. Compute a loss by comparing the prediction

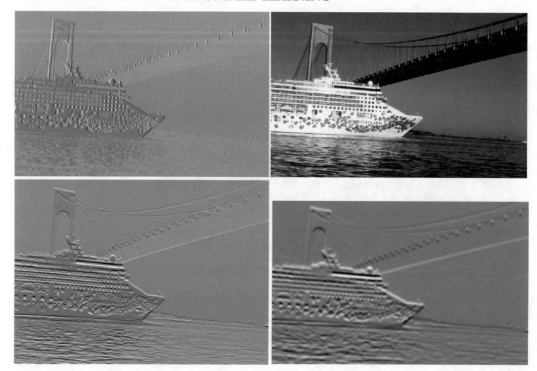

Figure A.8: The result of convolving an image (upper left) with three different filters. The filters perform Gaussian blurring and difference filtering. The direction of the gradient is either horizontal (upper left) or vertical (lower left). The receptive field (filter size) is 5×5 in the (upper left and lower left) but is increased to 25×25 for the lower right feature map that has a larger spatial extent of blurring. Notice that the choice of filter determines which image features are emphasized. In this example we chose the filters, in deep learning the filter coefficients are learned in the network training.

$\hat{Y}$ to the ground truth labels Y. Update all weights of the network (via backpropagation) to reduce the loss, then repeat the process until the loss has been reduced sufficiently.

One question is how to change the weights to make the predicted labels match the actual labels. (Note that brute-force trial and error won't work because of the large number of weights). Recall that the network is simply a function (albeit a very complicated function) and that this function can be expressed as a composition of functions For example $f(X, W) = f1(f2(f3(f4(X, W))))$, where X is the input and W are the weights. In general, the function is chosen to be differentiable so that gradient-based optimization can be used. For fixed input, the network function depends on W, the weights. For gradient descent, the weights at iteration 1, $W1$, depends on the prior weight $W0$ as follows: $W1 = W0 - \alpha \nabla(f(X, W0))$, where α

is a step size parameter. The gradient is computed using the chain rule for gradients via back-propagation.

Modern deep learning networks combine multiple layers, nonlinear functions called ReLu (rectified linear units), pooling, and sampling at particular layers. Examples of modern deep learning networks include Alexnet [115], Resnet [88], R-CNN [74, 168], VGGnet [193], and GANs [78]. The question of which deep learning architecture is best is an open research problem. Few theoretical results are available to guide the architecture choice. Unlike SVM and logistic regression, finding the parameters in deep learning is not a convex optimization problem. Non-convex optimization can be done with a technique called stochastic gradient descent (SGD). Recent research determines conditions for the local minimum of a non-convex problem to be a global minimizer [83]. This work is a step toward a more theoretical understanding of deep neural nets needed to move beyond the current "black box" approach.

A.3   ALEXNET, DENSE-NET, RES-NETS, AND ALL THAT

While deep learning shows the virtues of learned filter coefficients, the architectures of the networks are currently hand-crafted resulting in an everchanging landscape of best architecture designs. An important unsolved issue is how to choose among these architectures. As a sampling we discuss the architectures of three popular networks that provides insight to the general themes of deep learning network designs.

Alexnet   Alexnet [115] is a convolutional neural net (CNN) that started the current wave of deep learning approaches. It's architecture is made up of convolutional layers followed by a fully connected layer. There is a softmax function that maps the output of the last fully connected layer to a probability value. The last layer of the network has N nodes where N is the number of classes. The softmax function is given by

$$p_j(z) = \exp^{z_j} / \sum_k \exp^{z_k}, \tag{A.7}$$

where z_j indicates the jth node value. The softmax function takes a vector z of node values and transforms each element to a probability, a value in the range of 0–1 and summing to 1.

Residual Networks   Residual networks (Res-nets) have become very popular and typically surpass the performance of Alexnet by significantly increasing the depth of the network. The hypothesis in resnet is that a residual mapping is easier to fit. That is, if $H(X)$ is the function that the network achieves for input X, let $F(x) := H(x) - x$. Then $H(x) = F(x) + x$. This leads to a residual block as illustrated in Figure A.9. Resnet achieved an error of 3.57% on the Imagenet dataset by using 152 layers and became the ILSVRC and COCO 2015 competition winners. While learning improves with more layers, res-net is not simply an augmentation of CNNs with more layers. The problem is vanishing and exploding gradients that ruin the optimization. Batch normalization [98] is not a sufficient fix for these very deep networks. Res-net employs short-cut connections. The original idea came from multi-layer perceptrons when a linear layer connecting from the network input directly to the output was added.

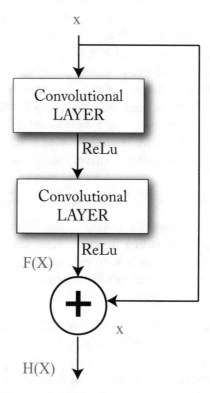

Figure A.9: Residual block is Res-net [88] that has a skip connection from the input to output. This block is one component in the network with typical instanteations from 18–151 layers.

Densely Connected Networks   Densely Connected Networks is an architecture that has similarities to the skip connections in Res-net. In Dense-net, connections between preceding layers are fed to all subsequent layers in a particular module as illustrated in Figure A.10. The full network typically has many dense blocks with convolutional and pooling layers between each block. In Res-net, the output at a particular layer depends on the prior layer and the input. In Dense-net, the output of a particular layer in the block depends on all prior layers. The feature maps are concatenated Dense-net achieved popularity as the CVPR 2017 best paper award [94].

SUMMARY

In this chapter we have discussed a high-level, basic introduction to deep learning. The chapter serves as a first step to more thorough investigation into deep learning networks.

Dense Block

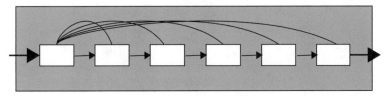

Figure A.10: Dense block is Dense-net [94] that has a dense connections to subsequent layers. This block is one component in the larger network.

PROBLEMS

A.1. For this problem, we consider simple scene classification using color histograms. Obtain a histogram of 50 images from two scene classes (e.g., urban and rural). Use approximately the same number of images for each class. Classify the images using only on the histograms of one color channel. The input are $N \times 1$ vectors where N is the number of histogram bins.

A.2. Train a logistic regression network to classify this data.

A.3. Train a multilayer perceptron to classify this data. Compare the results.

A.4. Train a support vector machine by providing color input for pixels from a "tomato" (class 1) and an "apple" (class 0). The feature vectors for the input points are the 3×1 color pixel values from known tomato and apple regions. Classify unlabeled "tomato" and "apple" regions. Compare this with a simple threshold distance algorithm to show the superiority of the SVM.

A.5. Use Keras or another machine learning library to implement a CNN similar to Alexnet and test on images from the Imagenet database.

Bibliography

[1] National Geographic. Patterns in nature. http://photography.nationalgeographic.com/photography/patterns-in-nature/ 1

[2] National Geographic. Patterns in nature. Exhibit, 2016. https://www.umass.edu/events/exhibit-patterns-nature

[3] John A. Adam. *Mathematics in Nature: Modeling Patterns in the Natural World*. Princeton University Press, 2006. 1

[4] Harsh Agrawal, Clint Solomon Mathialagan, Yash Goyal, Neelima Chavali, Prakriti Banik, Akrit Mohapatra, Ahmed Osman, and Dhruv Batra. CloudCV: Large scale distributed computer vision as a cloud service. *ArXiv Preprint ArXiv:1506.04130*, 2015. DOI: 10.1007/978-3-319-24702-1_11. 60

[5] George A. Alvarez, Representing multiple object as an ensemble enhances visual cognition, *Trends in Cognitive Sciences*, 15(3):122–131, 2011. DOI: 10.1016/j.tics.2011.01.003 7

[6] Relja Arandjelovic and Andrew Zisserman. All about VLAD. In *Computer Vision and Pattern Recognition (CVPR), Conference on*, pages 1578–1585, IEEE, 2013. DOI: 10.1109/cvpr.2013.207. 16

[7] Relja Arandjelovic and Andrew Zisserman. All about VLAD. In *Computer Vision and Pattern Recognition (CVPR), Conference on*, pages 1578–1585, IEEE, 2013. DOI: 10.1109/cvpr.2013.207. 19

[8] Pablo Arbelaez, Michael Maire, Charles Fowlkes, and Jitendra Malik. Contour detection and hierarchical image segmentation. *IEEE Transactions on Pattern Analysis and Machine Intelligence*, 33(5):898–916, 2011. DOI: 10.1109/tpami.2010.161. 26

[9] Dan Ariely. Seeing sets: Representation by statistical properties. *Psychology Science*, 12(2):157–162, 2001. DOI: 10.1111/1467-9280.00327 7

[10] Michael Ashikhmin. Synthesizing natural textures. In *Proc. of the Symposium on Interactive 3D Graphics, (I3D'01)*, pages 217–226, 2001. DOI: 10.1145/364338.364405. 47

[11] Mathieu Aubry, Sylvain Paris, Samuel W. Hasinoff, Jan Kautz, and Frédo Durand. Fast local Laplacian filters: Theory and applications. *ACM Transactions on Graphics*, 33(5):167:1–167:14, September 2014. DOI: 10.1145/2629645. 52

[12] Vijay Badrinarayanan, Alex Kendall, and Roberto Cipolla. Segnet: A deep convolutional encoder-decoder architecture for image segmentation. *IEEE Transactions on Pattern Analysis and Machine Intelligence*, 39(12):2481–2495, 2017. DOI: 10.1109/tpami.2016.2644615. 32

[13] Philip Ball. *Patterns in Nature: Why the Natural World Looks the Way it Does*. University of Chicago Press, 2016. DOI: 10.7208/chicago/9780226332567.001.0001. 1

[14] Mayank Bansal, Kostas Daniilidis, and Harpreet Sawhney. Ultrawide baseline facade matching for geo-localization. In *Large-Scale Visual Geo-Localization*, pages 77–98, Springer, 2016. DOI: 10.1007/978-3-319-25781-5_5. 61

[15] Z. Bar-Joseph, R. El-Yaniv, D. Lischinski, and M. Werman. Texture mixing and texture movie synthesis using statistical learning. *IEEE Transactions on Visualization and Computer Graphics*, 7(2):120–135, April 2001. DOI: 10.1109/2945.928165. 39

[16] Connelly Barnes, Eli Shechtman, Adam Finkelstein, and Dan B. Goldman. Patchmatch: A randomized correspondence algorithm for structural image editing. *ACM Transactions on Graphics*, 28(3):24:1–24:11, July 2009. DOI: 10.1145/1531326.1531330. 47

[17] Adela Barriuso and Antonio Torralba. Notes on image annotation. *CoRR*, abs/1210.3448, 2012. 36

[18] Sean Bell, Paul Upchurch, Noah Snavely, and Kavita Bala. Opensurfaces: A richly annotated catalog of surface appearance. *ACM Transactions on Graphics (TOG)*, 32(4):111, 2013. DOI: 10.1145/2461912.2462002. 21, 22

[19] Sean Bell, Paul Upchurch, Noah Snavely, and Kavita Bala. Material recognition in the wild with the materials in context database (supplemental material). In *Computer Vision and Pattern Recognition (CVPR)*, IEEE, 2015. DOI: 10.1109/cvpr.2015.7298970. 21, 22

[20] J. R. Bergen and B. Julesz. Rapid discrimination of visual patterns. *IEEE Transactions on Systems, Man, and Cybernetics*, SMC-13(5):857–863, September 1983. DOI: 10.1109/tsmc.1983.6313080. 11

[21] James R. Bergen and Bela Julesz. Parallel vs. serial processing in rapid pattern discrimination. *Nature*, 303(5919):696–698, 1983. DOI: 10.1038/303696a0. 11

[22] Christopher M. Bishop. *Pattern Recognition and Machine Learning (Information Science and Statistics)*. Springer-Verlag, New York, Inc., Secaucus, NJ, 2006. 65

[23] J. S. De Bonet and P. Viola. Texture recognition using a non-parametric multi-scale statistical model. In *Proc. of the IEEE Computer Society Conference on Computer Vision and Pattern Recognition (Cat. No.98CB36231)*, pages 641–647, June 1998. DOI: 10.1109/cvpr.1998.698672. 18

[24] Yuri Y. Boykov and M.-P. Jolly. Interactive graph cuts for optimal boundary and region segmentation of objects in ND images. In *Computer Vision, (ICCV). Proc. of the 8th IEEE International Conference on*, vol. 1, pages 105–112, 2001. DOI: 10.1109/iccv.2001.937505. 26, 29

[25] Scott Camazine. *Natural History*, pages 34–41, June 2003. 1

[26] Scott Camazine. *Self-Organization in Biological Systems*. Princeton University Press, 2003. 1

[27] Neill D. F. Campbell, Kartic Subr, and Jan Kautz. Fully-connected CRFS with non-parametric pairwise potential. In *Proc. of the IEEE Conference on Computer Vision and Pattern Recognition*, pages 1658–1665, 2013. DOI: 10.1109/cvpr.2013.217. 31, 32

[28] H. Chang, M. K. Ng, and T. Zeng. Reducing artifacts in JPEG decompression via a learned dictionary. *IEEE Transactions on Signal Processing*, 62(3):718–728, February 2014. DOI: 10.1109/tsp.2013.2290508. 56

[29] Dongdong Chen, Lu Yuan, Jing Liao, Nenghai Yu, and Gang Hua. Stylebank: An explicit representation for neural image style transfer. In *IEEE Conference on Computer Vision and Pattern Recognition (CVPR)*, 2017. DOI: 10.1109/cvpr.2017.296. 43, 48

[30] L. C. Chen, G. Papandreou, I. Kokkinos, K. Murphy, and A. L. Yuille. Deeplab: Semantic image segmentation with deep convolutional nets, atrous convolution, and fully connected CRFS. *IEEE Transactions on Pattern Analysis and Machine Intelligence*, 40(4):834–848, April 2018. DOI: 10.1109/tpami.2017.2699184. 32, 37

[31] Liang-Chieh Chen, Jonathan T. Barron, George Papandreou, Kevin Murphy, and Alan L. Yuille. Semantic image segmentation with task-specific edge detection using CNNs and a discriminatively trained domain transform. *CoRR*, abs/1511.03328, 2015. DOI: 10.1109/cvpr.2016.492. 32

[32] Liang-Chieh Chen, George Papandreou, Iasonas Kokkinos, Kevin Murphy, and Alan L. Yuille. Semantic image segmentation with deep convolutional nets and fully connected CRFS. *ArXiv Preprint ArXiv:1412.7062*, 2014. 32

[33] Liang-Chieh Chen, George Papandreou, Iasonas Kokkinos, Kevin Murphy, and Alan L. Yuille. Semantic image segmentation with deep convolutional nets and fully connected CRFS. *CoRR*, abs/1412.7062, 2014. 34

[34] Liang-Chieh Chen, George Papandreou, Florian Schroff, and Hartwig Adam. Rethinking atrous convolution for semantic image segmentation. *ArXiv Preprint ArXiv:1706.05587*, 2017. 32

[35] Sang Chul Chong and Anne Treisman. Representation of statistical properties. *Vision Research*, 43(4):393–404, 2003. DOI: 10.1016/S0042-6989(02)00596-5. 7

[36] Mircea Cimpoi, Subhransu Maji, Iasonas Kokkinos, Sammy Mohamed, and Andrea Vedaldi. Describing textures in the wild. In *The IEEE Conference on Computer Vision and Pattern Recognition (CVPR)*, June 2014. DOI: 10.1109/cvpr.2014.461. 4, 21

[37] Mircea Cimpoi, Subhransu Maji, Iasonas Kokkinos, and Andrea Vedaldi. Deep filter banks for texture recognition, description, and segmentation. *International Journal of Computer Vision*, 118(1):65–94, 2016. DOI: 10.1007/s11263-015-0872-3. 4

[38] Mircea Cimpoi, Subhransu Maji, and Andrea Vedaldi. Deep filter banks for texture recognition and segmentation. In *Proc. of the IEEE Conference on Computer Vision and Pattern Recognition*, pages 3828–3836, 2015. DOI: 10.1109/cvpr.2015.7299007. 16, 21

[39] Dorin Comaniciu and Peter Meer. Robust analysis of feature spaces: Color image segmentation. In *Computer Vision and Pattern Recognition, Proc. of the IEEE Computer Society Conference on*, pages 750–755, 1997. DOI: 10.1109/cvpr.1997.609410. 26, 29

[40] Dorin Comaniciu and Peter Meer. Mean shift: A robust approach toward feature space analysis. *IEEE Transactions on Pattern Analysis and Machine Intelligence*, 24(5):603–619, 2002. DOI: 10.1109/34.1000236. 26, 29

[41] Marius Cordts, Mohamed Omran, Sebastian Ramos, Timo Rehfeld, Markus Enzweiler, Rodrigo Benenson, Uwe Franke, Stefan Roth, and Bernt Schiele. The cityscapes dataset for semantic urban scene understanding. In *Proc. of the IEEE Conference on Computer Vision and Pattern Recognition (CVPR)*, 2016. DOI: 10.1109/cvpr.2016.350. 59

[42] Timothee Cour, Florence Benezit, and Jianbo Shi. Spectral segmentation with multiscale graph decomposition. In *Computer Vision and Pattern Recognition, (CVPR). IEEE Computer Society Conference on*, vol. 2, pages 1124–1131, 2005. DOI: 10.1109/cvpr.2005.332. 29

[43] Gabriella Csurka, Christopher R. Dance, Lixin Fan, Jutta Willamowski, and Cédric Bray. Visual categorization with bags of keypoints. In *Workshop on Statistical Learning in Computer Vision, (ECCV)*, pages 1–22, 2004. 18

[44] O. G. Cula and K. J. Dana. Compact representation of bidirectional texture functions. *IEEE Conference on Computer Vision and Pattern Recognition*, 1:1041–1067, December 2001. DOI: 10.1109/cvpr.2001.990645. 17, 18

[45] O. G. Cula and K. J. Dana. Image-based skin analysis. *Texture*, pages 35–41, June 2002. 18

[46] O. G. Cula, K. J. Dana, F. P. Murphy, and B. K. Rao. Skin texture modeling. *International Journal of Computer Vision*, 62(1/2):97–119, April/May 2005. DOI: 10.1023/b:visi.0000046591.79973.6f. 55

[47] Oana G. Cula and Kristin J. Dana. Compact representation of bidirectional texture functions. In *Computer Vision and Pattern Recognition, (CVPR). Proc. of the IEEE Computer Society Conference on*, vol. 1, pages I–I, 2001. DOI: 10.1109/cvpr.2001.990645. 42

[48] Oana G. Cula and Kristin J. Dana. 3D texture recognition using bidirectional feature histograms. *International Journal of Computer Vision*, 59(1):33–60, 2004. DOI: 10.1023/b:visi.0000020670.05764.55. 18

[49] O. G. Cula, K. J. Dana, F. P. Murphy, and B. K. Rao. Bidirectional imaging and modeling of skin texture. *IEEE Transactions on Biomedical Engineering*, 51(12):2148–2159, December 2004. DOI: 10.1109/tbme.2004.836520. 55

[50] Jifeng Dai, Kaiming He, and Jian Sun. Convolutional feature masking for joint object and stuff segmentation. In *Proc. of the IEEE Conference on Computer Vision and Pattern Recognition*, pages 3992–4000, 2015. DOI: 10.1109/cvpr.2015.7299025. 34

[51] K. J. Dana. Capturing computational appearance: More than meets the eye. *IEEE Signal Processing Magazine*, 33(5):70–80, September 2016. DOI: 10.1109/msp.2016.2580179. 22

[52] Kristin J. Dana, Shree K. Nayar, Bram Van Ginneken, and Jan J. Koenderink. Reflectance and texture of real-world surfaces. In *Computer Vision and Pattern Recognition, Proc. of the IEEE Computer Society Conference on*, pages 151–157, 1997. DOI: 10.1109/cvpr.1997.609313. 22

[53] Kristin J. Dana, Bram Van Ginneken, Shree K. Nayar, and Jan J. Koenderink. Reflectance and texture of real-world surfaces. *ACM Transactions on Graphics (TOG)*, 18(1):1–34, 1999. DOI: 10.1145/300776.300778. 22

[54] J. S. Debonet. Multiresolution sampling procedure for analysis and synthesis of texture images. *SIGGRAPH*, 1997. DOI: 10.1145/258734.258882. 39

[55] Jia Deng, Wei Dong, Richard Socher, Li-Jia Li, Kai Li, and Li Fei-Fei. Imagenet: A large-scale hierarchical image database. In *Computer Vision and Pattern Recognition, (CVPR). IEEE Conference on*, pages 248–255, 2009. DOI: 10.1109/cvpr.2009.5206848. 20

[56] Emily L. Denton, Soumith Chintala, Arthur Szlam, and Rob Fergus. Deep generative image models using a Laplacian pyramid of adversarial networks. In C. Cortes, N. D. Lawrence, D. D. Lee, M. Sugiyama, and R. Garnett, Eds., *Advances in Neural Information Processing Systems 28*, pages 1486–1494, Curran Associates, Inc., 2015. 52

[57] Jana Diesner, Terrill L. Frantz, and Kathleen M. Carley. Communication networks from the Enron email corpus "It's always about the people. Enron is no different?" *Computational and Mathematical Organization Theory*, 11(3):201–228, 2005. DOI: 10.1007/s10588-005-5377-0. 59

[58] Lourens Van Dijk, Ulrich W. Paetzold, Gerhard A. Blab, Ruud E. I. Schropp, and Marcel Vece. 3D-printed external light trap for solar cells. *Progress in Photovoltaics: Research and Applications*, 2015. DOI: 10.1002/pip.2702. 57

[59] Piotr Dollár, Ron Appel, Serge Belongie, and Pietro Perona. Fast feature pyramids for object detection. *IEEE Transactions on Pattern Analysis and Machine Intelligence*, 36(8):1532–1545, 2014. DOI: 10.1109/tpami.2014.2300479. 51

[60] Alexey Dosovitskiy and Thomas Brox. Generating images with perceptual similarity metrics based on deep networks. In D. D. Lee, M. Sugiyama, U. V. Luxburg, I. Guyon, and R. Garnett, Eds., *Advances in Neural Information Processing Systems 29*, pages 658–666, Curran Associates, Inc., 2016. 54

[61] Alexei A. Efros and William T. Freeman. Image quilting for texture synthesis and transfer. In *Proc. of the 28th Annual Conference on Computer Graphics and Interactive Techniques*, pages 341–346, ACM, 2001. DOI: 10.1145/383259.383296. 40, 41

[62] Alexei A. Efros and William T. Freeman. Image quilting for texture synthesis and transfer. In *Proc. of the 28th Annual Conference on Computer Graphics and Interactive Techniques, (SIGGRAPH'01)*, pages 341–346, New York, NY, ACM, 2001. DOI: 10.1145/383259.383296. 47

[63] Alexei A. Efros and Thomas K. Leung. Texture synthesis by non-parametric sampling. In *Computer Vision, Proc. of the 7th IEEE International Conference on*, vol. 2, pages 1033–1038, 1999. DOI: 10.1109/iccv.1999.790383. 40, 41

[64] Andre Esteva, Brett Kuprel, Roberto A. Novoa, Justin Ko, Susan M. Swetter, Helen M. Blau, and Sebastian Thrun. Dermatologist-level classification of skin cancer with deep neural networks. *Nature*, 542(7639):115–118, 2017. DOI: 10.1038/nature21056. 55

[65] Luc M. J. Florack, Bart M. ter Haar Romeny, Jan J. Koenderink, and Max A. Viergever. Scale and the differential structure of images. *Image and Vision Computing*, 10(6):376–388, 1992. DOI: 10.1016/0262-8856(92)90024-w. 15

[66] I. Fogel and D. Sagi. Gabor filters as texture discriminator. *Biological Cybernetics*, 61(2):103–113, June 1989. DOI: 10.1007/bf00204594. 13

[67] Balaji Ganeshan, Sandra Abaleke, R. C. Young, Christopher R. Chatwin, and Kenneth A. Miles. Texture analysis of non-small cell lung cancer on unenhanced computed tomography: Initial evidence for a relationship with tumour glucose metabolism

and stage. *Cancer Imaging*, 10(1):137–143, 2010. DOI: 10.1102/1470-7330.2010.0021. 55

[68] Balaji Ganeshan, Katherine Burnand, Rupert Young, Chris Chatwin, and Kenneth Miles. Dynamic contrast-enhanced texture analysis of the liver: Initial assessment in colorectal cancer. *Investigative Radiology*, 46(3):160–168, 2011. DOI: 10.1097/rli.0b013e3181f8e8a2. 55

[69] Balaji Ganeshan, Vicky Goh, Henry C. Mandeville, Quan Sing Ng, Peter J. Hoskin, and Kenneth A. Miles. Non-small cell lung cancer: Histopathologic correlates for texture parameters at CT. *Radiology*, 266(1):326–336, 2013. DOI: 10.1148/radiol.12112428. 55

[70] Leon Gatys, Alexander S. Ecker, and Matthias Bethge. Texture synthesis using convolutional neural networks. In *Advances in Neural Information Processing Systems*, pages 262–270, 2015. 42, 44, 47

[71] Leon A. Gatys, Alexander S. Ecker, and Matthias Bethge. Image style transfer using convolutional neural networks. In *Proc. of the IEEE Conference on Computer Vision and Pattern Recognition*, pages 2414–2423, 2016. DOI: 10.1109/cvpr.2016.265. 42, 47, 49

[72] A. Geiger, P. Lenz, and R. Urtasun. Are we ready for autonomous driving? The kitti vision benchmark suite. In *IEEE Conference on Computer Vision and Pattern Recognition*, pages 3354–3361, June 2012. DOI: 10.1109/cvpr.2012.6248074. 59

[73] Golnaz Ghiasi and Charless C. Fowlkes. Laplacian pyramid reconstruction and refinement for semantic segmentation. In *European Conference on Computer Vision*, pages 519–534. Springer, 2016. DOI: 10.1007/978-3-319-46487-9_32. 32, 52

[74] Ross Girshick, Jeff Donahue, Trevor Darrell, and Jitendra Malik. Rich feature hierarchies for accurate object detection and semantic segmentation. In *Proc. of the IEEE Conference on Computer Vision and Pattern Recognition*, pages 580–587, 2014. DOI: 10.1109/cvpr.2014.81. 34, 73

[75] Ross Girshick, Jeff Donahue, Trevor Darrell, and Jitendra Malik. Region-based convolutional networks for accurate object detection and segmentation. *IEEE Transactions on Pattern Analysis and Machine Intelligence*, 38(1):142–158, 2016. DOI: 10.1109/tpami.2015.2437384. 34

[76] Miltos Gletsos, Stavroula G. Mougiakakou, George K. Matsopoulos, Konstantina S. Nikita, Alexandra S. Nikita, and Dimitrios Kelekis. A computer-aided diagnostic system to characterize CT focal liver lesions: Design and optimization of a neural network classifier. *IEEE Transactions on Information Technology in Biomedicine*, 7(3):153–162, 2003. DOI: 10.1109/titb.2003.813793. 55

[77] Yunchao Gong, Liwei Wang, Ruiqi Guo, and Svetlana Lazebnik. Multi-scale orderless pooling of deep convolutional activation features. In *European Conference on Computer Vision*, pages 392–407, Springer, 2014. DOI: 10.1007/978-3-319-10584-0_26. 21

[78] Ian Goodfellow, Jean Pouget-Abadie, Mehdi Mirza, Bing Xu, David Warde-Farley, Sherjil Ozair, Aaron Courville, and Yoshua Bengio. Generative adversarial nets. In *Advances in Neural Information Processing Systems*, pages 2672–2680, 2014. 43, 45, 73

[79] Kristen Grauman and Trevor Darrell. The pyramid match kernel: Discriminative classification with sets of image features. In *Computer Vision, (ICCV). 10th IEEE International Conference on*, vol. 2, pages 1458–1465, 2005. DOI: 10.1109/iccv.2005.239. 18, 34

[80] Michelle R. Greene and Aude Oliva. Recognition of natural scenes from global properties: Seeing forest without representing the trees. *Cognitive Psychology* 58(2):137–176, 2009. DOI: 10.1016/j.cogpsych.2008.06.001 7

[81] Gemunu H. Gunaratne, David K. Hoffman, and Donald J. Kouri. Characterizations of natural patterns. *Physical Review E*, 57:5146–5149, May 1998. DOI: 10.1103/physreve.57.5146. 1

[82] E. Hadjidemetriou, M. D. Grossberg, and S. K. Nayar. Multiresolution histograms and their use for recognition. *IEEE Transactions on Pattern Analysis and Machine Intelligence*, 26(7):831–847, July 2004. DOI: 10.1109/tpami.2004.32. 18

[83] Benjamin Haeffele, Eric Young, and Rene Vidal. Structured low-rank matrix factorization: Optimality, algorithm, and applications to image processing. In *Proc. of the 31st International Conference on Machine Learning (ICML-14)*, pages 2007–2015, 2014. 73

[84] Michal Haindl and Jiří Filip. Visual acquisition. *Visual Texture*, pages 23–62, 2013. 22

[85] Denis Hamad and Philippe Biela. Introduction to spectral clustering. In *Information and Communication Technologies: From Theory to Applications, (ICTTA). 3rd International Conference on*, pages 1–6, IEEE, 2008. DOI: 10.1109/ictta.2008.4529994. 26

[86] K. He, X. Zhang, S. Ren, and J. Sun. Spatial pyramid pooling in deep convolutional networks for visual recognition. *IEEE Transactions on Pattern Analysis and Machine Intelligence*, 37(9):1904–1916, September 2015. DOI: 10.1109/tpami.2015.2389824. 51

[87] Kaiming He, Xiangyu Zhang, Shaoqing Ren, and Jian Sun. Spatial pyramid pooling in deep convolutional networks for visual recognition. In *European Conference on Computer Vision*, pages 346–361, Springer, 2014. DOI: 10.1007/978-3-319-10578-9_23. 34

[88] Kaiming He, Xiangyu Zhang, Shaoqing Ren, and Jian Sun. Deep residual learning for image recognition. In *The IEEE Conference on Computer Vision and Pattern Recognition (CVPR)*, June 2016. DOI: 10.1109/cvpr.2016.90. 20, 73, 74

[89] Xuming He, Richard S. Zemel, and Miguel Á Carreira-Perpiñán. Multiscale conditional random fields for image labeling. In *Computer Vision and Pattern Recognition, (CVPR). Proc. of the IEEE Computer Society Conference on*, vol. 2, pages II–II, 2004. DOI: 10.1109/cvpr.2004.1315232. 31

[90] David J. Heeger and James R. Bergen. Pyramid-based texture analysis/synthesis. In *Proc. of the 22nd Annual Conference on Computer Graphics and Interactive Techniques*, pages 229–238, ACM, 1995. DOI: 10.1145/218380.218446. 39, 42, 45

[91] Aaron Hertzmann, Charles E. Jacobs, Nuria Oliver, Brian Curless, and David H. Salesin. Image analogies. In *Proc. of the 28th Annual Conference on Computer Graphics and Interactive Techniques, (SIGGRAPH'01)*, pages 327–340, New York, NY, ACM, 2001. DOI: 10.1145/383259.383295. 47

[92] Michael M. Hoffman, Orion J. Buske, Jie Wang, Zhiping Weng, Jeff A. Bilmes, and William Stafford Noble. Unsupervised pattern discovery in human chromatin structure through genomic segmentation. *Nature Methods*, 9(5):473–476, 2012. DOI: 10.1038/nmeth.1937. 53

[93] Guoqiang Hu, Wee Peng Tay, and Yonggang Wen. Cloud robotics: Architecture, challenges and applications. *IEEE Network*, 26(3), 2012. DOI: 10.1109/mnet.2012.6201212. 61

[94] Gao Huang, Zhuang Liu, Kilian Q. Weinberger, and Laurens Van Der Maaten. Densely connected convolutional networks. In *Proc. of the IEEE Conference on Computer Vision and Pattern Recognition*, no. 2, page 3, 2017. DOI: 10.1109/cvpr.2017.243. 74, 75

[95] Xun Huang and Serge Belongie. Arbitrary style transfer in real-time with adaptive instance normalization. *ArXiv Preprint ArXiv:1703.06868*, 2017. DOI: 10.1109/iccv.2017.167. 43

[96] Xun Huang, Yixuan Li, Omid Poursaeed, John Hopcroft, and Serge Belongie. Stacked generative adversarial networks. *ArXiv*, 2016. DOI: 10.1109/cvpr.2017.202. 43

[97] Wei-Chih Hung, Yi-Hsuan Tsai, Xiaohui Shen, Zhe L. Lin, Kalyan Sunkavalli, Xin Lu, and Ming-Hsuan Yang. Scene parsing with global context embedding. *IEEE International Conference on Computer Vision (ICCV)*, pages 2650–2658, 2017. DOI: 10.1109/iccv.2017.287. 36

[98] Sergey Ioffe and Christian Szegedy. Batch normalization: Accelerating deep network training by reducing internal covariate shift. *ArXiv Preprint ArXiv:1502.03167*, 2015. 73

[99] A. Islam, S. M. S. Reza, and K. M. Iftekharuddin. Multifractal texture estimation for detection and segmentation of brain tumors. *IEEE Transactions on Biomedical Engineering*, 60(11):3204–3215, November 2013. DOI: 10.1109/tbme.2013.2271383. 55

[100] Anil K. Jain, Nalini K. Ratha, and Sridhar Lakshmanan. Object detection using gabor filters. *Pattern Recognition*, 30(2):295–309, 1997. DOI: 10.1016/s0031-3203(96)00068-4. 13

[101] Hervé Jégou, Matthijs Douze, Cordelia Schmid, and Patrick Pérez. Aggregating local descriptors into a compact image representation. In *Computer Vision and Pattern Recognition (CVPR), IEEE Conference on*, pages 3304–3311, 2010. DOI: 10.1109/cvpr.2010.5540039. 16, 19

[102] Justin Johnson, Alexandre Alahi, and Li Fei-Fei. Perceptual losses for real-time style transfer and super-resolution. In *European Conference on Computer Vision*, 2016. DOI: 10.1007/978-3-319-46475-6_43. 47, 49

[103] Bela Julesz. Experiments in the visual perception of texture. *Scientific American*, 232:34–43, 1975. DOI: 10.1038/scientificamerican0475-34. 12

[104] Bela Julesz and James R. Bergen. Textons, the fundamental elements in preattentive vision and perception of textures. *Bell System Technical Journal*, 1983. 11

[105] H. Jégou, M. Douze, C. Schmid, and P. Pérez. Aggregating local descriptors into a compact image representation. In *IEEE Computer Society Conference on Computer Vision and Pattern Recognition*, pages 3304–3311, June 2010. DOI: 10.1109/cvpr.2010.5540039. 16

[106] H. Jégou, M. Douze, C. Schmid, and P. Pérez. Aggregating local descriptors into a compact image representation. In *IEEE Computer Society Conference on Computer Vision and Pattern Recognition*, pages 3304–3311, June 2010. DOI: 10.1109/cvpr.2010.5540039. 20

[107] Nancy Kanwisher, Josh McDermott, and Marvin M. Chun. The fusiform face area: A module in human extrastriate cortex specialized for face perception. *Journal of Neuroscience*, 17(11):4302–4311, 1997. DOI: 10.1523/jneurosci.17-11-04302.1997. 48

[108] Daniel Kappler, Jeannette Bohg, and Stefan Schaal. Leveraging big data for grasp planning. In *Robotics and Automation (ICRA), IEEE International Conference on*, pages 4304–4311, 2015. DOI: 10.1109/icra.2015.7139793. 61

[109] Parneet Kaur, Kristin Dana, and Hang Zhang. Photo-realistic facial texture transfer, arXiv preprint https://arxiv.org/abs/1706.04306, 2017. 48, 50

[110] Ben Kehoe, Sachin Patil, Pieter Abbeel, and Ken Goldberg. A survey of research on cloud robotics and automation. *IEEE Transactions on Automation Science and Engineering*, 12(2):398–409, 2015. DOI: 10.1109/tase.2014.2376492. 61

[111] Bryan Klimt and Yiming Yang. The enron corpus: A new dataset for email classification research. In *European Conference on Machine Learning*, pages 217–226, Springer, 2004. DOI: 10.1007/978-3-540-30115-8_22. 59

[112] Felix Knöppel, Keenan Crane, Ulrich Pinkall, and Peter Schröder. Stripe patterns on surfaces. *ACM Transactions on Graphics*, 34(4):39:1–39:11, July 2015. DOI: 10.1145/2767000. 3

[113] Jan J. Koenderink. The structure of images. *Biological Cybernetics*, 50(5):363–370, 1984. DOI: 10.1007/bf00336961. 13, 15

[114] Vladlen Koltun. Efficient inference in fully connected CRFS with gaussian edge potentials. *Advances in Neural Information Processing Systems*, 2(3):4, 2011. 29

[115] Alex Krizhevsky, Ilya Sutskever, and Geoffrey E. Hinton. Imagenet classification with deep convolutional neural networks. In *Advances in Neural Information Processing Systems*, pages 1097–1105, 2012. DOI: 10.1145/3065386. 20, 73

[116] Philipp Krähenbühl and Vladlen Koltun. Efficient inference in fully connected CRFS with gaussian edge potentials. *Advances in Neural Information Processing Systems*, 2(3):4, 2011. 32

[117] R. Kumar, K. Dana, P. Anandan, N. Okamoto, J. Bergen, P. Hemler, T. S. Sumanaweera, P. A. van den Elsen, and J. Adler. Frameless registration of MR and CT 3D volumetric data sets. In *Proc. of IEEE Workshop on Applications of Computer Vision*, pages 240–248, December 1994. DOI: 10.1109/acv.1994.341316. 55

[118] Ľubor Ladický, Chris Russell, Pushmeet Kohli, and Philip H. S. Torr. Inference methods for CRFS with co-occurrence statistics. *International Journal of Computer Vision*, 103(2):213–225, 2013. DOI: 10.1007/s11263-012-0583-y. 31

[119] Lubor Ladicky, Jianbo Shi, and Marc Pollefeys. Pulling things out of perspective. In *Proc. of the IEEE Conference on Computer Vision and Pattern Recognition*, pages 89–96, 2014. DOI: 10.1109/cvpr.2014.19. 19

[120] L. Ladick, C. Russell, P. Kohli, and P. H. S. Torr. Associative hierarchical CRFS for object class image segmentation. In *IEEE 12th International Conference on Computer Vision*, pages 739–746, September 2009. DOI: 10.1109/iccv.2009.5459248. 32

[121] John Lafferty, Andrew McCallum, Fernando Pereira, et al. Conditional random fields: Probabilistic models for segmenting and labeling sequence data. In *Proc. of the 18th International Conference on Machine Learning, (ICML)*, vol. 1, pages 282–289, 2001. 19, 29, 31

[122] S. Lazebnik, C. Schmid, and J. Ponce. Beyond bags of features: Spatial pyramid matching for recognizing natural scene categories. In *IEEE Computer Society Conference on Computer Vision and Pattern Recognition (CVPR'06)*, vol. 2, pages 2169–2178, 2006. DOI: 10.1109/cvpr.2006.68. 18, 34, 51

[123] Svetlana Lazebnik, Cordelia Schmid, and Jean Ponce. A sparse texture representation using affine-invariant regions. In *Computer Vision and Pattern Recognition. Proc. of the IEEE Computer Society Conference on*, vol. 2, pages II–II, 2003. DOI: 10.1109/cvpr.2003.1211486. 18

[124] Svetlana Lazebnik, Cordelia Schmid, and Jean Ponce. A sparse texture representation using local affine regions. *IEEE Transactions on Pattern Analysis and Machine Intelligence*, 27(8):1265–1278, 2005. DOI: 10.1109/tpami.2005.151. 18

[125] Y. LeCun, B. Boser, J. S. Denker, D. Henderson, R. E. Howard, W. Hubbard, and L. D. Jackel. Handwritten digit recognition with a back-propagation network. In *Neural Information Processing Systems (NIPS)*, 1989. 20

[126] P. S. Lee, H.R . Piehler, B. L. Adams, G. Jarvis, H. Hampel, and A. D. Rollett. Influence of surface texture on orange peel in aluminum. *Journal of Materials Processing Technology*, 80:315–319, 1998. DOI: 10.1016/s0924-0136(98)00189-7. 56

[127] Seungkyu Lee, Yanxi Liu, and Robert Collins. Shape variation-based frieze pattern for robust gait recognition. In *Computer Vision and Pattern Recognition, (CVPR'07). IEEE Conference on*, pages 1–8, 2007. DOI: 10.1109/cvpr.2007.383138. 4

[128] R. M. Lehman, R. S. Mezrich, R. Kumar, K. Dana, and P. Anandan. Frameless three-dimensional volume registration for stereotactic planning. *Stereotactic and Functional Neurosurgery*, 66(1):153–153, 1996. 55

[129] Thomas Leung and Jitendra Malik. Representing and recognizing the visual appearance of materials using three-dimensional textons. *International Journal of Computer Vision*, 43(1):29–44, 2001. DOI: 10.1023/A:1011126920638. 17, 18, 42

[130] Sergey Levine, Peter Pastor, Alex Krizhevsky, and Deirdre Quillen. Learning hand-eye coordination for robotic grasping with deep learning and large-scale data collection. *ArXiv Preprint ArXiv:1603.02199*, 2016. DOI: 10.1177/0278364917710318. 61

[131] Chuan Li and Michael Wand. Precomputed real-time texture synthesis with markovian generative adversarial networks. In Bastian Leibe, Jiri Matas, Nicu Sebe, and Max Welling, Eds., *Computer Vision (ECCV)*, pages 702–716, Cham, Springer International Publishing, 2016. DOI: 10.1007/978-3-319-46454-1. 44

[132] Guosheng Lin, Anton Milan, Chunhua Shen, and Ian Reid. Refinenet: Multi-path refinement networks for high-resolution semantic segmentation. In *IEEE Conference on Computer Vision and Pattern Recognition (CVPR)*, 2017. DOI: 10.1109/cvpr.2017.549. 36

[133] Guosheng Lin, Chunhua Shen, Anton van den Hengel, and Ian Reid. Efficient piece-wise training of deep structured models for semantic segmentation. In *Proc. of the IEEE Conference on Computer Vision and Pattern Recognition*, pages 3194–3203, 2016. DOI: 10.1109/cvpr.2016.348. 32

[134] Huang-Yu Lin, Sheng-Wen Wang, Chien-Chung Lin, Zong-Yi Tu, Po-Tsung Lee, Huang-Ming Chen, and Hao-Chung Kuo. Effective optimization and analysis of white led properties by using nano-honeycomb patterned phosphor film. *Optics Express*, 24(17):19032–19039, 2016. DOI: 10.1364/oe.24.019032. 56

[135] T. Y. Lin, P. Dollár, R. Girshick, K. He, B. Hariharan, and S. Belongie. Feature pyramid networks for object detection. In *IEEE Conference on Computer Vision and Pattern Recognition (CVPR)*, pages 936–944, July 2017. DOI: 10.1109/cvpr.2017.106. 51

[136] Tsung-Yu Lin and Subhransu Maji. Visualizing and understanding deep texture representations. In *Computer Vision and Pattern Recognition (CVPR)*, 2016. DOI: 10.1109/cvpr.2016.305. 21

[137] Tsung-Yu Lin, Aruni RoyChowdhury, and Subhransu Maji. Bilinear CNN models for fine-grained visual recognition. In *International Conference on Computer Vision (ICCV)*, 2015. DOI: 10.1109/iccv.2015.170. 21

[138] Tsung-Yu Lin, Aruni RoyChowdhury, and Subhransu Maji. Bilinear CNNs for fine-grained visual recognition. In *Transactions of Pattern Analysis and Machine Intelligence (PAMI)*, 2017. 21

[139] Yanxi Liu, Yanghai Tsin, and Wen-Chieh Lin. The promise and perils of near-regular texture. *International Journal of Computer Vision*, 62(1):145–159, 2005. DOI: 10.1023/b:visi.0000046593.03875.01. 3

[140] J. Long, E. Shelhamer, and T. Darrell. Fully convolutional networks for semantic segmentation. In *IEEE Conference on Computer Vision and Pattern Recognition (CVPR)*, pages 3431–3440, June 2015. DOI: 10.1109/cvpr.2015.7298965. 32, 34

[141] David G. Lowe. Distinctive image features from scale-invariant key-points. *International Journal of Computer Vision*, 60(2):91–110, 2004. DOI: 10.1023/b:visi.0000029664.99615.94. 15

[142] Fujun Luan, Sylvain Paris, Eli Shechtman, and Kavita Bala. Deep photo style transfer. *CoRR*, abs/1703.07511, 2017. DOI: 10.1109/cvpr.2017.740. 48

[143] Robert J. Maciunas, Robert L. Galloway, Jr., and Jim W. Latimer. The application accuracy of stereotactic frames. *Neurosurgery*, 35(4):682–695, 1994. DOI: 10.1097/00006123-199410000-00015. 55, 56

[144] Siddharth K. Madan, Kristin J. Dana, and Oana G. Cula. Quasiconvex alignment of multimodal skin images for quantitative dermatology. In *Computer Vision and Pattern Recognition Workshops. IEEE Computer Society Conference on*, pages 117–124, 2009. DOI: 10.1109/cvpr.2009.5204346. 55

[145] Will Maddern, Geoffrey Pascoe, Chris Linegar, and Paul Newman. 1 year, 1,000 km: The Oxford robotcar dataset. *The International Journal of Robotics Research*, 36(1):3–15, 2017. DOI: 10.1177/0278364916679498. 59

[146] Vashisht Madhavan and Trevor Darrell. The BDD-nexar collective: A large-scale, crowd-sourced, dataset of driving scenes. Master's thesis, EECS Department, University of California, Berkeley, May 2017. 59

[147] A. Mahendran and A. Vedaldi. Understanding deep image representations by inverting them. *IEEE Conference on Computer Vision and Pattern Recognition (CVPR)*, pages 5188–5196, June 2015. DOI: 10.1109/cvpr.2015.7299155. 48

[148] Michael Maire, Takuya Narihira, and Stella X. Yu. Affinity CNN: Learning pixel-centric pairwise relations for figure/ground embedding. In *Proc. of the IEEE Conference on Computer Vision and Pattern Recognition*, pages 174–182, 2016. DOI: 10.1109/cvpr.2016.26. 36

[149] Michael Maire and Stella X. Yu. Progressive multigrid eigensolvers for multiscale spectral segmentation. In *Proc. of the IEEE International Conference on Computer Vision*, pages 2184–2191, 2013. DOI: 10.1109/iccv.2013.272. 29

[150] Jitendra Malik, Serge Belongie, Thomas Leung, and Jianbo Shi. Contour and texture analysis for image segmentation. *International Journal of Computer Vision*, 43(1):7–27, June 2001. DOI: 10.1007/978-1-4615-4413-5_9. 13, 17

[151] Jitendra Malik and Pietro Perona. Preattentive texture discrimination with early vision mechanisms, *Journal of the Optical Society of America A*, 7(5):923–932, May 1990. DOI: 10.1364/JOSAA.7.000923 11

[152] A. Mansoor, U. Bagci, Z. Xu, B. Foster, K. N. Olivier, J. M. Elinoff, A. F. Suffredini, J. K. Udupa, and D. J. Mollura. A generic approach to pathological lung segmentation. *IEEE Transactions on Medical Imaging*, 33(12):2293–2310, December 2014. DOI: 10.1109/tmi.2014.2337057. 55

[153] M. L. Miranda-Medina, P. Somkuti, D. Bianchi, U. Cihak-Bayr, D. Bader, M. Jech, and A. Vernes. Characterisation of orange peel on highly polished steel surfaces. *Surface Engineering*, 31(7):519–525, 2015. DOI: 10.1179/1743294414y.0000000407. 56

[154] Gary Monheit, Armand B. Cognetta, Laura Ferris, Harold Rabinovitz, Kenneth Gross, Mary Martini, James M. Grichnik, Martin Mihm, Victor G. Prieto, Paul Googe, et al. The performance of melafind: A prospective multicenter study. *Archives of Dermatology*, 147(2):188–194, 2011. DOI: 10.1001/archdermatol.2010.302. 55

[155] Sandy A. Napel, Christopher F. Beaulieu, Cesar Rodriguez, Jingyu Cui, Jiajing Xu, Ankit Gupta, Daniel Korenblum, Hayit Greenspan, Yongjun Ma, and Daniel L. Rubin. Automated retrieval of CT images of liver lesions on the basis of image similarity: Method and preliminary results 1. *Radiology*, 256(1):243–252, 2010. DOI: 10.1148/radiol.10091694. 55

[156] Hyeonwoo Noh, Seunghoon Hong, and Bohyung Han. Learning deconvolution network for semantic segmentation. In *Proc. of the IEEE International Conference on Computer Vision*, pages 1520–1528, 2015. DOI: 10.1109/iccv.2015.178. 32, 34

[157] T. Ojala, M. Pietikainen, and T. Maenpaa. Multiresolution gray-scale and rotation invariant texture classification with local binary patterns. *IEEE Transactions on Pattern Analysis and Machine Intelligence*, 24(7):971–987, July 2002. DOI: 10.1109/tpami.2002.1017623. 18

[158] A. Owens, P. Isola, J. McDermott, A. Torralba, E. H. Adelson, and W. T. Freeman. Visually indicated sounds. In *IEEE Conference on Computer Vision and Pattern Recognition (CVPR)*, pages 2405–2413, June 2016. DOI: 10.1109/cvpr.2016.264. 22

[159] Devi Parikh and Kristen Grauman. Relative attributes. In *Computer Vision (ICCV), IEEE International Conference on*, pages 503–510, 2011. DOI: 10.1109/iccv.2011.6126281. 56

[160] F. Perronnin and C. Dance. Fisher kernels on visual vocabularies for image categorization. In *IEEE Conference on Computer Vision and Pattern Recognition*, pages 1–8, June 2007. DOI: 10.1109/cvpr.2007.383266. 19

[161] Florent Perronnin, Jorge Sánchez, and Thomas Mensink. Improving the fisher kernel for large-scale image classification. In *European Conference on Computer Vision*, pages 143–156, Springer, 2010. DOI: 10.1007/978-3-642-15561-1_11. 16

[162] Florent Perronnin, Jorge Sánchez, and Thomas Mensink. Improving the fisher kernel for large-scale image classification. In *Proc. of the 11th European Conference on Computer Vision: Part IV, (ECCV'10)*, pages 143–156, Springer-Verlag, Berlin, Heidelberg, 2010. DOI: 10.1007/978-3-642-15561-1_11. 20

[163] J. B. Peter and E. H. Adelson. The Laplacian pyramid as a compact image code. *IEEE Transactions on Communications*, 31:532–540, 1983. DOI: 10.1515/9781400827268.28. 13, 18, 39, 51

[164] Pedro O. Pinheiro, Tsung-Yi Lin, Ronan Collobert, and Piotr Dollár. Learning to refine object segments. In *European Conference on Computer Vision*, pages 75–91, Springer, 2016. DOI: 10.1007/978-3-319-46448-0_5. 51

[165] Javier Portilla and Eero P. Simoncelli. A parametric texture model based on joint statistics of complex wavelet coefficients. *International Journal of Computer Vision*, 40(1):49–70, 2000. DOI: 10.1023/A:1026553619983. 39, 42, 44

[166] Alec Radford, Luke Metz, and Soumith Chintala. Unsupervised representation learning with deep convolutional generative adversarial networks. *ArXiv Preprint ArXiv:1511.06434*, 2015. 43, 44

[167] A. Ravichandran, R. Chaudhry, and R. Vidal. Categorizing dynamic textures using a bag of dynamical systems. *IEEE Transactions on Pattern Analysis and Machine Intelligence*, 35(2):342–353, February 2013. DOI: 10.1109/tpami.2012.83. 18

[168] Shaoqing Ren, Kaiming He, Ross Girshick, and Jian Sun. Faster R-CNN: Towards real-time object detection with region proposal networks. In *Advances in Neural Information Processing Systems*, pages 91–99, 2015. DOI: 10.1109/tpami.2016.2577031. 73

[169] Laura Walker Renninger and Jitendra Malik. When is scene identification just texture recognition? *Vision Research*, 44(19):2301–2311, 2004. DOI: 10.1016/s0042-6989(04)00191-9. 17

[170] Bart M. Ter Haar Romeny and Luc Florack. A multiscale geometric model of human vision. In *The Perception of Visual Information*, pages 73–114, Springer, 1993. DOI: 10.1007/978-1-4612-1836-4_4. 15

[171] Frank Rosenblatt. The perceptron: A probabilistic model for information storage and organization in the brain. *Psychological Review*, 65(6):386, 1958. DOI: 10.1037/h0042519. 65

[172] Carsten Rother, Vladimir Kolmogorov, and Andrew Blake. Grabcut: Interactive foreground extraction using iterated graph cuts. *ACM Transactions on Graphics*, 23(3):309–314, 2004. DOI: 10.1145/1015706.1015720. 26, 29

[173] Ryan Rowe, German Creamer, Shlomo Hershkop, and Salvatore J. Stolfo. Automated social hierarchy detection through email network analysis. In *Proc. of the 9th WebKDD and 1st SNA-KDD Workshop on Web Mining and Social Network Analysis*, pages 109–117, ACM, 2007. DOI: 10.1145/1348549.1348562. 53

[174] Bryan C. Russell, Antonio Torralba, Kevin P. Murphy, and William T. Freeman. Labelme: A database and web-based tool for image annotation. *International Journal of Computer Vision*, 77(1):157–173, May 2008. DOI: 10.1007/s11263-007-0090-8. 36

[175] Chris Russell, Pushmeet Kohli, Philip H. S. Torr, et al. Associative hierarchical CRFS for object class image segmentation. In *Computer Vision, IEEE 12th International Conference on*, pages 739–746, 2009. 29

[176] H. Sadeghi, S. Valaee, and S. Shirani. 2dtripnp: A robust two-dimensional method for fine visual localization using Google streetview database. *IEEE Transactions on Vehicular Technology*, (99):1–1, 2016. DOI: 10.1109/tvt.2016.2615630. 61

[177] Alexandria Sage. Where's the lane? Self-driving cars confused by shabby US rodways. Reuters, Los Angeles, California, 2016. 57

[178] P. Saisan, G. Doretto, Ying Nian Wu, and S. Soatto. Dynamic texture recognition. In *Proc. of the IEEE Computer Society Conference on Computer Vision and Pattern Recognition, (CVPR)*, vol. 2, pages II–58–II–63, 2001. DOI: 10.1109/cvpr.2001.990925. 18

[179] N. Saranjam, S. Chandra, J. Mostaghimi, H. Fan, and J. Simmer. Orange peel formation due to surface tension-driven flows within drying paint films. *Journal of Coatings Technology and Research*, 13(3):413–426, 2016. DOI: 10.1007/s11998-015-9752-6. 56

[180] C. Schmid. Constructing models for content-based image retrieval. In *Proc. of the IEEE Computer Society Conference on Computer Vision and Pattern Recognition, (CVPR)*, vol. 2, pages II–39–II–45, 2001. DOI: 10.1109/cvpr.2001.990922. 18

[181] Gabriel Schwartz and Ko Nishino. Visual material traits: Recognizing per-pixel material context. In *Computer Vision Workshops (ICCVW), IEEE International Conference on*, pages 883–890, 2013. DOI: 10.1109/iccvw.2013.121. 22

[182] Gabriel Schwartz and Ko Nishino. Automatically discovering local visual material attributes. In *Proc. of the IEEE Conference on Computer Vision and Pattern Recognition*, pages 3565–3573, 2015. DOI: 10.1109/cvpr.2015.7298979. 22, 56

[183] Gabriel Schwartz and Ko Nishino. Discovering perceptual attributes in a deep local material recognition network. *ArXiv Preprint ArXiv:1604.01345*, 2016. 22

[184] Gabriel Schwartz and Ko Nishino. Material recognition from local appearance in global context. *ArXiv Preprint ArXiv:1611.09394*, 2016. 22

[185] Ahmed Selim, Mohamed Elgharib, and Linda Doyle. Painting style transfer for head portraits using convolutional neural networks. *ACM Transactions on Graphics*, 35(4):129:1–129:18, July 2016. DOI: 10.1145/2897824.2925968. 48

[186] E. Shelhamer, J. Long, and T. Darrell. Fully convolutional networks for semantic segmentation. *IEEE Transactions on Pattern Analysis and Machine Intelligence*, 39(4):640–651, April 2017. DOI: 10.1109/tpami.2016.2572683. 32

[187] Jitesh Shetty and Jafar Adibi. Discovering important nodes through graph entropy the case of enron email database. In *Proc. of the 3rd International Workshop on Link Discovery*, pages 74–81, ACM, 2005. DOI: 10.1145/1134271.1134282. 59

[188] Jianbo Shi and Jitendra Malik. Normalized cuts and image segmentation. *IEEE Transactions on Pattern Analysis and Machine Intelligence*, 22(8):888–905, 2000. DOI: 10.1109/34.868688. 26, 29

[189] Yi-Chang Shih, Sylvain Paris, Connelly Barnes, William T. Freeman, and Frédo Durand. Style transfer for headshot portraits. *SIGGRAPH*, 2014. DOI: 10.1145/2601097.2601137. 48

[190] J. Shotton, M. Johnson, and R. Cipolla. Semantic texton forests for image categorization and segmentation. In *IEEE Conference on Computer Vision and Pattern Recognition*, pages 1–8, June 2008. DOI: 10.1109/cvpr.2008.4587503. 18

[191] Jamie Shotton, John Winn, Carsten Rother, and Antonio Criminisi. Textonboost: Joint appearance, shape and context modeling for multi-class object recognition and segmentation. In *European Conference on Computer Vision*, pages 1–15, Springer, 2006. DOI: 10.1007/11744023_1. 19, 29

[192] Eero P. Simoncelli and William T. Freeman. The steerable pyramid: A flexible architecture for multi-scale derivative computation. In *Image Processing, Proc. of the International Conference on*, vol. 3, pages 444–447, IEEE, 1995. DOI: 10.1109/icip.1995.537667. 39

[193] K. Simonyan and A. Zisserman. Very deep convolutional networks for large-scale image recognition. *CoRR*, abs/1409.1556, 2014. 73

[194] Peter S. Stevens. Patterns in nature. 1974. 1

[195] Asman Tamang, Aswin Hongsingthong, Porponth Sichanugrist, Vladislav Jovanov, Makoto Konagai, and Dietmar Knipp. Light-trapping and interface morphologies of amorphous silicon solar cells on multiscale surface textured substrates. *IEEE Journal of Photovoltaics*, 4(1):16–21, 2014. DOI: 10.1109/jphotov.2013.2280020. 56

[196] Joshua B. Tenenbaum and William T. Freeman. Separating style and content. In *Proc. of the 9th International Conference on Neural Information Processing Systems, (NIPS'96)*, pages 662–668, Cambridge, MA, MIT Press, 1996. 21

[197] Joshua B. Tenenbaum and William T. Freeman. Separating style and content with bilinear models. *Neural Computation*, 12(6):1247–1283, 2000. DOI: 10.1162/089976600300015349. 21

[198] Joshua B. Tenenbaum and William T. Freeman. Separating style and content with bilinear models. *Neural Computation*, 12(6):1247–1283, June 2000. DOI: 10.1162/089976600300015349. 47

[199] W. S. Tong, C. K. Tang, M. S. Brown, and Y. Q. Xu. Example-based cosmetic transfer. In *Computer Graphics and Applications, (PG'07). 15th Pacific Conference on*, pages 211–218, October 2007. DOI: 10.1109/pg.2007.31. 47

[200] Fatima Toor, Howard M. Branz, Matthew R. Page, Kim M. Jones, and Hao-Chih Yuan. Multi-scale surface texture to improve blue response of nanoporous black silicon solar cells. *Applied Physics Letters*, 99(10):103501, 2011. DOI: 10.1063/1.3636105. 56

[201] A. Treisman. Preattentive processing in vision. *Computer Vision, Graphics, and Image Processing*, 31(2):156–177, 1985. DOI: 10.1016/s0734-189x(85)80004-9. 11

[202] Greg Turk. Generating textures on arbitrary surfaces using reaction-diffusion. *ACM SIGGRAPH Computer Graphics*, 25(4):289–298, 1991. DOI: 10.1145/127719.122749. 3

[203] Mark R. Turner. Texture discrimination by Gabor functions. *Biological Cybernetics*, 55(2):71–82, 1986. DOI: 10.1007/BF00341922. 13

[204] D. Ulyanov, A. Vedaldi, and V. Lempitsky. Improved texture networks: Maximizing quality and diversity in feed-forward stylization and texture synthesis. In *IEEE Conference on Computer Vision and Pattern Recognition (CVPR)*, pages 4105–4113, July 2017. DOI: 10.1109/cvpr.2017.437. 44

[205] Dmitry Ulyanov, Vadim Lebedev, Andrea Vedaldi, and Victor Lempitsky. Texture networks: Feed-forward synthesis of textures and stylized images. In *International Conference on Machine Learning (ICML)*, 2016. 4, 43, 45, 47

[206] Paul Upchurch, Jacob Gardner, Geoff Pleiss, Robert Pless, Noah Snavely, Kavita Bala, and Kilian Q. Weinberger. Deep feature interpolation for image content changes. In *The IEEE Conference on Computer Vision and Pattern Recognition (CVPR)*, July 2017. DOI: 10.1109/cvpr.2017.645. 48

[207] Jan C. Van Gemert, Jan-Mark Geusebroek, Cor J. Veenman, and Arnold W. M. Smeulders. Kernel codebooks for scene categorization. In *European Conference on Computer Vision*, pages 696–709, Springer, 2008. DOI: 10.1007/978-3-540-88690-7_52. 19

[208] M. Varma and A. Zisserman. Texture classification: Are filter banks necessary? In *IEEE Computer Society Conference on Computer Vision and Pattern Recognition, Proc.*, vol. 2, pages II–691–698, June 2003. DOI: 10.1109/cvpr.2003.1211534. 18

[209] Manik Varma and Andrew Zisserman. A statistical approach to texture classification from single images. *International Journal of Computer Vision*, 62(1):61–81, April 2005. DOI: 10.1023/b:visi.0000046589.39864.ee. 17

[210] Ulrike Von Luxburg. A tutorial on spectral clustering. *Statistics and Ccomputing*, 17(4):395–416, 2007. DOI: 10.1007/s11222-007-9033-z. 26

[211] Hsin-Ping Wang, An-Cheng Li, Tzu-Yin Lin, and Jr-Hau He. Concurrent improvement in optical and electrical characteristics by using inverted pyramidal array structures toward efficient SI heterojunction solar cells. *Nano Energy*, 23:1–6, 2016. DOI: 10.1016/j.nanoen.2016.02.034. 56

[212] Geoffrey I. Webb. Discovering significant patterns. *Machine Learning*, 68(1):1–33, 2007. DOI: 10.1007/s10994-007-5006-x. 53

[213] Li-Yi Wei and Marc Levoy. Fast texture synthesis using tree-structured vector quantization. In *Proc. of the 27th Annual Conference on Computer Graphics and Interactive Techniques*, pages 479–488, ACM, Press/Addison-Wesley Publishing Co., 2000. DOI: 10.1145/344779.345009. 40

[214] Andrew Witkin and Michael Kass. Reaction-diffusion textures. *ACM SIGGRAPH Computer Graphics*, 25(4):299–308, 1991. DOI: 10.1145/127719.122750. 3

[215] Andrew P. Witkin. Scale space filtering. *Proc. of the International Joint Conference Artificial Intelligence*, pages 1019–1021, 1983. DOI: 10.1016/b978-0-08-051581-6.50036-2. 13

[216] N. J. Wittridge and R. D. Knutsen. A microtexture based analysis of the surface roughening behaviour of an aluminium alloy during tensile deformation. *Materials Science and Engineering: A*, 269(1):205–216, 1999. DOI: 10.1016/s0921-5093(99)00145-8. 56

[217] Franco Woolfe and Andrew Fitzgibbon. Shift-invariant dynamic texture recognition. *Computer Vision, (ECCV). 9th European Conference on Computer Vision, Proc. Part II*, pages 549–562, Graz, Austria, May 7–13, 2006. DOI: 10.1007/11744047_42. 18

[218] Wenqi Xian, Patsorn Sangkloy, Jingwan Lu, Chen Fang, Fisher Yu, and James Hays. Texturegan: Controlling deep image synthesis with texture patches. *CoRR*, abs/1706.02823, 2017. 44

[219] Jia Xue, Hang Zhang, Kristin Dana, and Ko Nishino. Differential angular imaging for material recognition. In *IEEE Conference on Computer Vision and Pattern Recognition (CVPR)*, vol. 5, 2017. DOI: 10.1109/cvpr.2017.734. 22

[220] Richard A. Young. *Gaussian derivative theory of spatial vision: Analysis of cortical cell receptive field line-weighting profiles.* General Motors Research Laboratories, 1985. 14

[221] Amir R. Zamir, Asaad Hakeem, Luc Van Gool, Mubarak Shah, and Richard Szeliski. Introduction to large-scale visual geo-localization. In *Large-Scale Visual Geo-Localization*, pages 1–18, Springer, 2016. DOI: 10.1007/978-3-319-25781-5_1. 61

[222] Matthew D. Zeiler, Graham W. Taylor, and Rob Fergus. Adaptive deconvolutional networks for mid and high level feature learning. In *Computer Vision (ICCV), IEEE International Conference on*, pages 2018–2025, 2011. DOI: 10.1109/iccv.2011.6126474. 32

[223] H. Zhang, J. Xue, and K. Dana. Deep ten: Texture encoding network. *IEEE Conference on Computer Vision and Pattern Recognition (CVPR)*, pages 2896–2905, July 2017. DOI: 10.1109/cvpr.2017.309. 4, 34

[224] Hang Zhang and Kristin Dana. Multi-style generative network for real-time transfer. *European Conference of Computer Vision Workshops (ECCVW)*, 2018. 43, 48, 49

[225] Hang Zhang, Kristin Dana, and Ko Nishino. Reflectance hashing for material recognition. In *Computer Vision and Pattern Recognition (CVPR), IEEE Conference on*, pages 3071–3080, 2015. DOI: 10.1109/cvpr.2015.7298926. 22

[226] Hang Zhang, Kristin Dana, and Ko Nishino. Friction from reflectance: Deep reflectance codes for predicting physical surface properties from one-shot in-field reflectance. In *European Conference on Computer Vision*, pages 808–824, Springer, 2016. DOI: 10.1007/978-3-319-46493-0_49. 22

[227] Hang Zhang, Kristin Dana, Jianping Shi, Zhongyue Zhang, Xiaogang Wang, Ambrish Tyagi, and Amit Agrawal. Context encoding for semantic segmentation. *IEEE Conference on Computer Vision and Pattern Recognition*, 2018. 16

[228] Hang Zhang, Kristin J. Dana, Jianping Shi, Zhongyue Zhang, Xiaogang Wang, Ambrish Tyagi, and Amit Agrawal. Context encoding for semantic segmentation. *IEEE Conference on Computer Vision and Pattern Recognition*, 2018. 34, 36, 37

[229] Hang Zhang, Jia Xue, and Kristin Dana. Deep ten: Texture encoding network. *IEEE Conference on Computer Vision and Pattern Recognition*, 2017. DOI: 10.1109/cvpr.2017.309. 16, 21

[230] J. Zhang, M. Marszałek, S. Lazebnik, and C. Schmid. Local features and kernels for classification of texture and object categories: A comprehensive study. *International Journal of Computer Vision*, 73(2):213–238, June 2007. DOI: 10.1109/cvprw.2006.121. 18

[231] H. Zhao, J. Shi, X. Qi, X. Wang, and J. Jia. Pyramid scene parsing network. In *IEEE Conference on Computer Vision and Pattern Recognition (CVPR)*, pages 6230–6239, July 2017. DOI: 10.1109/cvpr.2017.660. 52

[232] Hengshuang Zhao, Jianping Shi, Xiaojuan Qi, Xiaogang Wang, and Jiaya Jia. Pyramid scene parsing network. In *IEEE Conference on Computer Vision and Pattern Recognition (CVPR)*, pages 2881–2890, 2017. DOI: 10.1109/cvpr.2017.660. 34, 37

[233] Jianhua Zhao, Aihua Wang, Martin A. Green, and Francesca Ferrazza. 19.8% efficient "honeycomb" textured multicrystalline and 24.4% monocrystalline silicon solar cells. *Applied Physics Letters*, 73(14):1991–1993, 1998. 56

[234] Peng Zhao and Long Quan. Translation symmetry detection in a fronto-parallel view. In *Computer Vision and Pattern Recognition (CVPR), IEEE Conference on*, pages 1009–1016, 2011. DOI: 10.1109/cvpr.2011.5995482. 4

[235] Shuai Zheng, Sadeep Jayasumana, Bernardino Romera-Paredes, Vibhav Vineet, Zhizhong Su, Dalong Du, Chang Huang, and Philip H. S. Torr. Conditional random fields as recurrent neural networks. In *Proc. of the IEEE International Conference on Computer Vision*, pages 1529–1537, 2015. DOI: 10.1109/iccv.2015.179. 31, 32, 35

[236] Bolei Zhou, Hang Zhao, Xavier Puig, Sanja Fidler, Adela Barriuso, and Antonio Torralba. Scene parsing through ade20k dataset. In *Proc. CVPR*, 2017. DOI: 10.1109/cvpr.2017.544. 36

[237] Jun-Yan Zhu, Philipp Krähenbühl, Eli Shechtman, and Alexei A. Efros. Generative visual manipulation on the natural image manifold. In *European Conference on Computer Vision*, pages 597–613, Springer, 2016. DOI: 10.1007/978-3-319-46454-1_36. 44

[238] S. C. Zhu, Y. N. Wu, and D. Mumford. Filters, random field and maximum entropy: Towards a unified theory for texture modeling. *International Journal of Computer Vision*, 27(2):1–20, March/April 1998. DOI: 10.1023/A:1007925832420. 19, 39, 40

[239] Jana Zujovic, Thrasyvoulos N. Pappas, and David L. Neuhoff. Structural texture similarity metrics for image analysis and retrieval. *IEEE Transactions on Image Processing*, 22(7):2545–2558, 2013. DOI: 10.1109/tip.2013.2251645. 54

Author's Biography

KRISTIN J. DANA

Dr. Kristin J. Dana received a Ph.D. from Columbia University (New York, NY) in 1999, an M.S. degree from Massachusetts Institute of Technology in 1992 (Cambridge, MA), and a B.S. degree in 1990 from the Cooper Union (New York, NY). She is currently a Full Professor in the Department of Electrical and Computer Engineering at Rutgers University. She is also a member of the graduate faculty of Rutgers Computer Science Department. Prior to academia, Dr. Dana was on the research staff at Sarnoff Corporation a subsidiary of SRI (formerly Stanford Research Institute), developing real-time motion estimation algorithms for applications in defense, biomedicine, and entertainment industries. She is the recipient of the General Electric "Faculty of the Future" fellowship in 1990, the Sarnoff Corporation Technical Achievement Award in 1994 for the development of a practical algorithm for the real-time alignment of visible and infrared video images, the 2001 National Science Foundation Career Award for a program investigating surface science for vision and graphics, and a team recipient of the Charles Pankow Innovation Award in 2014 from the ASCE. Dr. Dana's research expertise is in computer vision including computational photography, machine learning, quantitative dermatology, illumination modeling, texture and reflectance models, optical devices, and applications of robotics. On these topics, she has published over 70 papers in leading journals and conferences.

Printed in the United States
by Baker & Taylor Publisher Services